RALPH BATES – SWINDON'S 'UNKNOWN' AUTHOR

GW01418637

Ralph Bates

~ Swindon's 'unknown' author ~

Michael Yates

ELSP

Published in 2014
by ELSP

www.ex-librisbooks.co.uk

Printed by
CPI Anthony Rowe
Chippenham, Wiltshire

ISBN 978-1-906641-74-0

All correspondence and enquiries regarding
this book please email the author,
Michael Yates at lokaart@aol.com

Contents

Introduction

In 1835 Isambard Kingdom Brunel began work on the Great Western Railway line from London to Bristol. For his headquarters, Brunel chose Swindon, in Wiltshire, then a small village on a hill, and the town that we know today grew from Brunel's factory and workshops, the "new town" slowly moving up the hill, street by street, until both "new town" and "old town" became one. The GWR factory employed hundreds of people and working conditions have been described in Alfred Williams' autobiographical book *Life in a Railway Factory*. Williams was working in the factory as a hammerman and he is known to have been working on the text in 1911. The book, he said, would be "a record of my experience in the workshop – strong, faithful pictures of the industrial life, rough and vigorous". Alfred Williams resigned from his job in 1914 and *Life in a Railway Factory* appeared in October, 1915. One commentator said that the book was "the most daring and comprehensive condemnation of factory life that had appeared in Europe for thirty years". Surprisingly, it appears that over the six year period following the book's publication only a dozen or so copies were actually sold in Swindon. Nevertheless Williams was proud of his achievement, saying that it was the only good book on factory life that we have in England written by a working man.

Alfred Williams, who became known as the "Hammerman Poet", spent the rest of his life as a writer, producing a number of fine books about the countryside around Swindon. He is, alongside Richard Jeffries, perhaps one of Swindon's best-known writers. But there was another writer who began his working life in the GWR factory. This was Ralph Bates and this is his story.

Early Days

Some people are born, work and die in the same place. Others, those with a restless spirit, make the world their home, and Swindon-born writer, political activist, soldier, mountaineer and University Professor, Ralph Bates, was one such person.

Ralph was born on the 3rd November 1899, at 15a, Morse Street, Swindon, Wiltshire. He was the first of four sons born to Henry Roy Bates, a "turner, fitter and lathe man" who worked in the GWR factory, and Mabel Stephens Bates, née Rosby. Henry and Mabel were married on 29th June 1898, at St Mark's Church in Swindon. Henry, then described as a "turner", was living at 2, Cromwell Street, Swindon, and was the son of Alfred William Bates, an engine fitter who also worked in the GWR factory. Mabel was then living at 36, Farringdon Street, Swindon, and was the daughter of William Ralph Rosby, who was also an engine fitter working in the GWR factory. Witnesses to the wedding were Alfred and Ann Bates, William Ralph and Lilly Nellie Rosby, and a George James Watts.

According to the 1901 census Henry and Mabel Bates were then living at 54, Morse Street, Swindon. Henry was 26 years old, Mabel was aged 23, Ralph was one year old and his brother, Roy Stephens Bates, was just one month old. Mabel's brother, Ralph W. Rosby, a twenty year old wood cabinet maker, was also living at the address. Ten years later the family had moved a short distance to 34, Farnsby Street, Swindon. Ralph Rosby was no longer living with the Bates, but there were two additional sons, Leslie Alfred Bates, then aged 1 year, and a newly born Ronald Bates. Interestingly, neither Ralph Bates nor any of his brothers are listed as having been baptized at St Mark's church, where their parents were married.

At some point or other Ralph and his family are believed to have lived on a farm, "in the Wiltshire Downs", further details being unknown. However, recent research in reference to Guernsey Farm,

Morse Street, Swindon, 1930s. Number 54 is the second house past the corner shop

a 94-acre farm just to the north-west of Swindon, shows that, "By 1901, several of the farm's cottage occupiers were employed by the Great West Railway".[1] But whether or not this was the farm in question remains a moot point.

Ralph was obviously a talented child – he played the organ in various churches while still a schoolboy – and may have attended the GWR School in College Street, not far from the GWR factory; although one account says that Ralph attended the "Swindon and North Wiltshire Secondary School" in Victoria Road, Swindon, where he became "fluent in French and Spanish".[2] This is almost certainly a reference to the Swindon and North Wiltshire Technical Institution, which opened on 27th January 1897. Until 1952 it housed both a technical college and a secondary school.

Swindon and North Wiltshire Technical Institution

Ralph may still have been at school when he joined a reading group that was organised by the Archdeacon of North Wiltshire, presumably Ravenscroft Stewart (1845–1921) who held that post from 1910 until 1919, and one book that Bates remembered was E. H. Spender's *Through the High Pyrenees*, published in 1898. This was the book that inspired Ralph Bates to later travel to France and Spain. Ralph began by writing poems and simple anecdotes, some of which were written for the *Daily Express* and the *Westminster Gazette*. One early poem 'The Comfort of Little Things' was printed in *Adelphi* magazine in 1925.

The Comfort of Little Things

How might I live within the empty stead
That memorably your laughter once had filled?
How might I endure, hearing still your tread?
So I have hastened to the lands untilled,
Among harsh sorrels I have laid my head.

How might I go upon accustomed hills?
Have I not said that from love's gleaming peaks
There flowed sweet nurture of the clear cold rills?
How might I go where still the old songs seek
My lips, how see the low slope's daffodils?

How may mine eyes look westward when the sun
Burns redly on the sea grown grey and dim?
Even so ends love, I said, that is begun
In that red glory of the eastern rim
Oh bitterness the world's large splendours, every one.

So I have found my peace in little things
That have not yet grown treasonable to me:
In a little gleaming shell with purple rings
Is comfort, and by the pale stones of the sea
I find my comfort when a small wave flings
The red dulse' sodden branch, green laver's veil.
Sea hollies and the spear-grass silver flecked
Are mine, for love large-striding hath not recked
These random things, and these things may not fail:
So have I found my peace in little things.

Many years later Ralph Bates produced the novel *The Dolphin in the Wood*, which contains this disclaimer, "This novel, although it is cast in the form of an autobiography, is wholly a work of the imagination and has no reference to any real persons, living or dead." The novel tells of a young man growing up in Wiltshire at the time of the First World War. Like Ralph Bates, he plays the church organ and is a poet.

Under the influence of William Butler Yeats…my poems were

11

filled with mystical remarks about glistening beetles in the dust and little shells with purple rings...Some were later published by John Middleton Murry in the *Adelphi*.[3]

John Middleton Murry was, indeed, the editor of the *Adelphi* and he did publish 'The Comfort of Little Things', with its line "a little gleaming shell with purple rings", so perhaps Ralph Bates's disclaimer should be taken with a pinch of salt.

On Monday, 20th November 1916 Ralph followed his father into the GWR factory, where he became an apprentice fitter, turner and erector in the factory's "B" shop, which housed the Erectors, Boilermakers and Painters. He became a member of the National Union of Railwaymen and remained in the Union for several years after he left the factory.[4] At one time Ralph was part of a group that restored the *Lady of Lyon*, one of the great locomotives designed by George Jackson Churchward. There is a story that Ralph was reported to have "climbed up the drive belts and control shafts of the machines after they were turned off for the weekend, to the overhead roof struts, before crawling along from strut to strut across the shop and returning to the floor level on the other side of "O" shop, the Tool Room." If this is true, then it was a precursor to his later mountain-climbing activities.[5]

Alfred Williams had already left the GWR factory when Ralph Bates began working there, but I do wonder, though, if the two knew each other. And did Ralph Bates ever read Alfred's book *Life in a Railway Factory*? I ask this, because, as we shall see later, Ralph became involved in left-wing union activity, and was Alfred Williams's book influential in making Ralph Bates the man that he became?

In 1916 Ralph Bates had volunteered for First World War service in the Royal Flying Corps. In *The Dolphin in the Wood*, he recounts the moment when he first became obsessed with the notion of flying.

One frosty Saturday morning I was walking across the floor of Starvall Coombe when something flashed white in the sky. An aeroplane was stunting at an enormous height. I watched it, wondering why the pilot was showing off his tricks to the bare heavens. Suddenly, as the plane described a long plunging arc and rolled over, my heart leapt with ambition. I must learn to fly. The Royal Flying Corps.[6]

Ralph Bates did apply to join the Royal Flying Corps, but, "I NEVER flew. After nine weeks of training in a Cadet Wing I was washed out at a medical examination".[7] Later, he said, "I was not intelligent enough to know that no working man would ever get a commission."

According to Paul Joseph Melia:

The strong sense of class prejudice that Bates felt in the Royal Flying Corps, which was "the beginning of my alienation", stemmed from the fact "I was not a gentleman and one or two courageous snobs in the Wing had let me know it". He used this to explain why he had not been chosen for flying duty. (Bates, 1950: pp. 76-8) What is significant in comparison to those writing from a theoretical Marxist standpoint is that its importance, the tragedy, does not exist much except at an individual level – no people are going to go hungry or otherwise suffer beyond the personal humiliation – and it has no Marxist terminology, yet it is still told from a Marxist perspective, describing a dialectical problem stemming from position in society and privilege.[8]

The one or two "snobs" may have been from the "personal friends, lads from Marlborough, Rugby, Eton and Harrow" who became "lines of silent attention ... from the circumference of foreign people to the centre, where I sat."[9] I find it interesting to note that Ralph Bates cites Marlborough School at the beginning of his list of public schools, because Marlborough lies only about ten miles to the south of Swindon and I do wonder if Ralph had previously come into contact with pupils from that school.

And Melia concludes:

> Bates' realization in the Royal Flying Corps can be inferred as the dawn of his Communist sensibility: "the beginning of my alienation" followed a transformation when "personal friends, lads from Marlborough, Rugby, Eton and Harrow" became "lines of silent attention ... from the circumference of foreign people to the centre, where I sat." Behind the politeness, perhaps even noblesse oblige, for the first time Bates perceived their ineluctable social difference, and ultimately that that social distinction was paramount.[10]

On 8th December 1917, Ralph entered the army serving as an infantryman with the 16th Queen's Royal West Surrey Regiment, becoming a lance corporal who taught soldiers how to deal with poison gas attacks. According to at least one source, Ralph Bates spent some time fighting in the trenches.[11] In 1918 he was arrested because he attended a meeting about the Russian revolution while wearing his army uniform. He was sentenced to two weeks on the parade ground, where he had to march around in full kit for six hours a day. "I decided then and there that my judgment of the officer class was just. I had met only one or two decent men, or at least who decently employed their power."

Many years later, in 1950, Ralph Bates included a section in *The Dolphin in the Wood* which deals with the narrator's cousin, Will, being court-martialled and executed by firing squad for striking an officer. According to the narrator:

And nothing, nothing could wipe out the guilt that lay at someone else's door, at a whole class of them, except they be swept away.[12]

Again, we can clearly see how Ralph Bates's First World War army experience also contributed to his nascent political beliefs.

After the war Ralph Bates returned to Swindon and re-entered the GWR factory on 30th November 1918, this time working in the Testing House. According to some sources, including a number of national newspaper obituaries, Ralph left the GWR factory sometime around 1923. According to an obituary in the *Guardian* newspaper:

> By 1923 he had joined the Communist party. But the childhood lure of further places was strong, and he was soon off to Paris, where he had a job as a street-cleaner. Then he worked his passage on a ship to Spain, where he bummed around, surviving on odd jobs.[13]

The same story is also related in the introduction to the 1986 reprint of Bates's novel *The Olive Field*.

> Bates had gone from his native England to Spain in the Twenties with the backing of the Communist International.[14]

According to H. Gustav Klaus:

> When in 1923 [Ralph Bates] chose a Continental place of residence, it was...Barcelona...From here he made regular excursions to the interior of Catalonia and the Pyrenees, becoming a passionate and experienced mountain climber.[15]

Gustav Klaus also adds that:

Bates lived in Barcelona and Sabadell until the early 'thirties, supporting himself by practicing the trade of fitter or turner, or working in the docks and as a fisherman.[16]

In fact, every person who has commented on this period of Ralph Bates's life says more or less the same. Namely, that Ralph left Swindon for Paris and Spain sometime around the early 1920s. Perhaps this is what Ralph told people. And the GWR Register of Workmen, a large leather-bound book containing handwritten entries, shows that Ralph Bates's apparent "final" payment was made on 3rd November, 1920.[17] But another document clearly shows that Ralph "resigned" from the GWR on Friday, 2nd May 1930. His weekly pay was then shown as 42/- per week.[18]

What probably happened was that the GWR changed its record-keeping to a card index system in 1920, and these cards have not survived. Anyone previously checking the GWR Register could easily have thought that the 1920 payment was Ralph Bates's final payment.

Sometime around 1923 Ralph began mixing with members of the Communist Party of Great Britain (CPGB). Harry Pollitt, later to become General Secretary of the party, was one such friend. It seems likely that Bates and Pollitt had first met because of a project to send British railway mechanics to the Soviet Union to help repair the country's railway system.

Several people have described Ralph Bates as being a member of the CPGB, although according to Dr Alan Munton, Bates "was never a card-carrying member of the Communist Party...In general he was not influenced by Marxism, but found William Morris, Keir Hardy and even Prince Kropokin, the anarchist theorist, more congenial."[19] H. Gustav Klaus agrees that Ralph was a "non-card carrying Communist" and sees him more as "a proletarian author, a practitioner of the political novel, a champion of the culture of the

(Spanish) common people".[20]

According to the writer of Ralph Bates's *Volunteer* obituary:

> Bates' membership in various Communist parties is not clear...
> He was close to the leader of the CPGB, Harry Pollitt, and in a
> conversation with me last year he still spoke very highly of Pollitt,
> but not so highly of the CPUSA (Communist Party of the USA) and
> its cadre. He was not impressed with the CPUSA, or its members
> with him. Many of the obituaries write that Bates left the party in
> 1939...but he was never really a joiner nor a follower, but rather a
> man of action and energy.[21]

If the GWR records are correct, then we must assume that
Ralph Bates left Swindon in the spring of 1930 and went to Spain,
perhaps stopping over in Paris where he possibly worked as a street
cleaner. Ralph then moved to Spain where he had a number of jobs.
At one point he spent some time working as a seaman and trade
union agitator in the docks of Catalonia (in one instance, while
working for the Spanish General Workers Union – *Unión General
de Trabajadores*, or UGT – he organized a union in a fish cannery),
before settling in the Pyrenees, where he discovered a passion for
mountain climbing, becoming, for a time, a guide. Apparently, the
start of the Spanish Civil War, in 1936, put paid to a growing idea that
Ralph had for writing a book on mountaineering. Ralph Bates often
said that his great-grandfather had a connection with Spain, having
been the owner and captain of a Spanish tramp steamer that carried
sherry and other goods around the Mediterranean, and Ralph said
that he first went to Spain in search of his great-grandfather's grave in
Cadiz. In his 1934 novel *Lean Men* the narrator leaves Wiltshire for
Spain, explaining that, "there was a ship-captain great-grandfather
Roy, buried in the civil cemetery at Cadiz".[22]

It must have been something of a shock to Ralph when he

arrived in Spain:

> For days there seemed to be two worlds, mine and this which I had now entered. Sometimes this new world seemed like a softly gliding picture, in which I could take part if I wished; at other times struggle was the picture, but far off and small.[23]

In the introduction to the book *Reporter in Spain* by "Frank Pitcairn" (actually Claude Cockburn) Ralph Bates describes a year that he (Bates) spent in Spain c.1930–31:

> Just before the monarchy fell I walked month after month, throughout a year, twelve hundred miles, through the immense, almost unknown, the "lost" Cordilleras of Spain, to find out how Spaniards live. I dare say that I know more about the life and work of Spanish shepherds, olive workers, ploughmen, peasants, than these Englishmen whom I find talking of a 'glorious Spanish tradition' and its fascist champions. I believe I know the real tradition, the way olives are grown, wine made, cork gathered, what songs are sung for the picking of figs, or the herding of cattle. I know because I have followed them, by what immemorial tracks the sheep flocks go up in summer from the red choking plains to the hills...I remember hearing a ploughing song...It was sung to me by a skull-faced man, a dried and ageing field-worker in Navalonquilla (sic), a starving village of the Avila Province. The words and the tune of his song, the very shape of his plough and the skill of his hands had come out of the Middle Age.[24]

Ralph Bates clearly witnessed a divided society during the year when he crisscrossed Spain on foot.

At Sietamo the peasants demanded winnowing machines of the advancing workers. Years ago I was in Javierrelatre, a village of High Aragon. There was a famine in Javierrelatre the year before, because no wind had blown to winnow the grain. Do you think the army of Spain, the corrupt, disloyal, illiterate generals, who could not defeat the armed Moors of the Riff without French aid and could not defeat the unarmed workers of Spain without Italian aid – do you think these men and the bankers, the political time-servers, the decaying aristocracy, the bishops, will understand about those winnowing machines?[25]

But Ralph Bates also sought a refuge where he could find the time to become a writer. He had, by this time, apparently married Winifred Sanford, born in 1898, who was teaching in London's east end when they met.[26] Winifred and her parents were loyal supporters of the Labour Party, although Winifred left the Labour Party and joined the Communist Party in 1934, when she became active in the "Friends of the Soviet Union", a CPGB "front" organization. She also supported the Worker's Birth Control Group and the Maternal Mortality Group and, on one occasion, probably in 1934, went to Paris as a delegate to a conference on Women Against War and Fascism.

Ralph began to settle down and write. Luckily he was encouraged in this by the writer and literary agent Edward Garnett, who, at the time, was working for the London publishing house Jonathan Cape. Garnett arranged to send £5 a week to Ralph so that he could complete his first book *Sierra*, a collection of short stories about the hardships of Spanish village life. The book was published in August, 1933, by Peter Davies of London. Both Ralph and Winifred had become fluent in Spanish and Catalan and the eleven stories are clearly written with an ear to these languages. One story, *The Quince*, begins thus:

Catarina Piver slowly tied up the remains of her meal of bread and sheep's milk cheese in her black kerchief and rose to her feet. The middle heat of day had passed and already there were little pitch-black shadows under the bulging walls of the red ravine in which her small patch of the Retaking lay. The cracked bell of the village above struck three as she hobbled out from the thin network shade of the olive tree and took up her hoe.

'A hard land, the ravine of Saint Pau de las Campanas,' she thought as she stood gazing down the gorge towards the ridge which, curving round, blocked the view out over the violet plain one could see from the village. 'And a hard piece, the field of the Retaking.'

A hard land. Upon the waterless shelves of dull red earth that lay below the monotonous cliffs nothing would grow, except box-shrubs, a few weakling pines, and here and there a moribund olivar. There was nothing to do on the Retaking, the onion crop was already dried by the long drought. She let her hoe fall and its smooth shaft polished by years of hard, cracked hands lay resting against her black dress.

Sierra was the first of Ralph's socialist realism novels. The final story, 'The Birth of a Man', ends with the death of republican sympathizers at the hands of civil guards:

God!

The branches were tumbling, the people frozen…hands raised… oh, horror! Horror!

Ear-splitting banging of rifles behind him.

Oh, most Holy Mother of God! Ah…a hurtling, invisible beam struck him in the leg; he fell; a child was flung down as if by a hurricane, skull smashed; screams and people falling like reeds before the shrieking, invisible rods that stabbed and hissed among them.

Ralph Bates later said that he had been influenced by "Catalonia in general and the Cerdanya in the Pyrenees in particular – as well as by the peasants and workers of the region." It has been suggested that he could have also been inspired by the works of the Spanish anarchist, (later communist), writer Ramón J. Sender (1901–1982), both writers sharing similar political beliefs and fictional themes, although Ralph denied this. He did, however, agree that he could have been influenced by the Spanish Catholic novelist José Maria de Pereda (1833–1906), even though their world views were very different.[27]

Sierra was followed by *Lean Men,* published in 1934 by Peter Davis, a novel that tells of a country in turmoil.[28] The story is that of an English Comintern agent, surely Ralph Bates himself, who is "up against an overwhelmingly cruel and powerful state" and the novel ends with a failed worker's uprising. On the title page of the novel Bates has added the quotation "Ripeness is all" from Shakespeare's *King Lear* (Act V. Scene II), and the phrase is repeated at the end of the novel in this passage:

> But Morality springs from within, is Life itself, answered conscience inflexibly.
>
> Within conscience itself was division, argument.
>
> Was this man's death justified? By the barest of margins, No. One must learn to stake one's life upon the barest of margins. That was ripeness, maturity. He knew now the meaning of those words, "Ripeness is all".

According to the *Manchester Guardian*, "[*Lean Men*] is a work of rich nature and of rare experiences; a book of force and beauty.... All who are interested in Spain and its present conditions should read it", while a reviewer in *The Observer* said that, "I shall be surprised if Ralph Bates does not prove himself, within the next ten years, one of the most remarkable and powerful contemporary English novelists".[29] An acclaimed biography of Franz Schubert appeared in the following year and both *Franz Schubert* and *Sierra* are dedicated to "Winifred and Rosaleen". Winifred was, of course, Ralph's wife, while Rosaleen was Rosaleen Ross (1909–2004), a communist who met Ralph and Winifred Bates in London and who later worked with Winifred during the Spanish Civil War.

It is interesting that Ralph Bates's only non-fiction book should be a biography of the Austrian composer Franz Schubert. Schubert, like Ralph Bates, came from a less privileged background and, again like Ralph, rebelled against the Church.[30] Schubert, however, did continue to compose for the Church and many of these works are truly sublime. As we have seen, Ralph Bates was an organist. He clearly loved music and the Schubert book could only have been written by a person well versed in the complexities of classical music. This is Bates's take on Schubert's Mass in F:

In 1814 Schubert composed his Mass in F, the first of six and the one in which he most nearly achieves the profoundest essence of catholic worship. That essence is, of course, not really expressible in accented and non-contrapuntal music, as doctors teach, though the Holy Ghost, presumably the inspirer of music, has not always been aware of the fact, to judge by the beauty of many of these non-polyphonic masses.

Several of Ralph Bates's novels contain musical references, usually to Beethoven, Mozart or, occasionally, Vaughan Williams or Stravinsky, though he does also mention English folk-dance tunes, such as *Sir Roger de Coverley, Black Jack, Sellinger's Round, Rufty-Tufty* and *Goddesses*, as well as the moralistic piece *Man's Life's a Vapour, Full of Woes*, which is sung as a round.[31] During the 1930s, 1940s and 1950s Ralph Bates also reviewed a number of music books for various publications.[32]

Ralph Bates's best-known book, *The Olive Field* appeared in 1936, published, this time by Jonathan Cape. This was, almost certainly, Ralph's finest book. "*The Olive Field* will last. It stands out among the 'proletarian' fiction of the 1930s as a revelatory and sympathetic inside story of people making a living on the edge."[33] For Ralph Bates, the olive tree held a special meaning:

> The olive tree had always been a symbol to me. Its "immobility in the sapless winter had been a reproach to man's embitterment"; its "sobriety of minute blossom had been a rebuke to licence." Its harvest at its richest was ever "a reproof to man avid of yield from the meagre tillage he gives to life." The olive tree was a symbol of austerity, of frugality..."[34]

The Olive Field tells the age-old story of two friends who fall in love with the same woman. It is set in rural Spain, a land of almost pagan customs, feudal landlords and a highly conservative catholic church. Bates's novel portrays the harshness and cruelty of the land and people. It stresses the suffering that constituted much of 1930s Spain.

> Bates keenly spells out the wildest of Spanish paradoxes, that in this ancient Christian country, the land of the olive and the olive branch, those most enduring Judaeo-Christian emblems of peace, there should be so much opposition to peacefulness, especially opposition based in Christian practice and observance.[35]

It is as though Ralph Bates was trying to find the *Duende*, that soul of Gypsy *Cante jondo*, that so fascinated the poet Frederico García Lorca.[36] Here is Bates's take on an evening in a café, the Miracle Court.

Ay!

At the long note the guitar swelled loudly and then was silent for a moment.

> Ay! When I saw sweet bread drawn out my thoughts
> to you this evening fled.

And as Caro continued with falling notes the guitar began to play isolated chords.

> And when they laid it on the white wood boards
> I thought of you, O woman, sweet as bread.

"Olé!" ejaculated Mudarra with quiet intensity.
"Ay!" began the singer again, and then he sang that she had the sweetness and the purity of the olives' press lying still in the wooden vats.
"Olé!" Mudarra ejaculated fiercely, beginning a glittering cadenza.

> Ay! Man liveth aye by bread and oil
> Man dies, they say, with oil and bread,

Caro began again, and with the last insistent but quiet phrases he told the woman that she was as bread and oil.
The guitar died away with the faintest touching of a high harmonic and the Court was silent.[37]

But *The Olive Field* is also about the changes that were occurring within Spain.

At midnight, general strike. At daybreak Civil War.[38]

The novel, like its predecessor *Lean Men*, ends with a failed protest. This time it the Asturian miners' strike of 1934, which quickly developed into a revolutionary uprising, one that was put down by the Spanish Navy and the Spanish Republican Army, using troops sent to Spain from Spanish Morocco by General Franco.

Many of the characters in *The Olive Field* are anarchists, and Bates could not resist comparing them to members of the Catholic Church. According to the novel's Communist, Robledo, "Anarchism is nothing more than Christianity without God". No wonder, when the Civil War began two years later, there was so much in-fighting between the various Left-wing factions! Apparently, Ralph Bates planned to write a sequel to *The Olive Field* but the coming of the Spanish Civil War put paid to that idea.[39]

Why did *The Olive Field* strike such a receptive chord in both Britain and America? German academic H. Gustav Klaus, while discussing Bates and another 1930s' writer, the Indian communist Mulk Raj Anand, offers this telling suggestion:

> The novels of Bates and Anand deal with the theme of exploitation and human resistance in places far removed from Britain, but their relevance for, and connection with, the struggle on the 'home front' must have been fairly obvious to readers in the thirties.[40]

Ralph Bates's next book, *Rainbow Fish – Four Short Novels* did not, however, gain the same respect as *The Olive Field*.

> "*Rainbow Fish – Four Short Novels* (1937), set widely across Europe, is far more ordinary; the shock mixture of Spanish violence, cruelty and utopian aspiration is clearly what Bates's imagination needed to thrive on."[41]

Civil War

Ralph Bates was in London during the period June 19th–23rd 1936, when he attended a meeting of the International Association of Writers for the Defence of Culture, held at Friends House. It was a closed meeting and only members of the Association were allowed to attend. Speakers included André Malraux, H. G. Wells, C. Day Lewis and Ernst Toller. A number of other speakers, including André Gide, Aldous Huxley, E. M. Forster and Virginia Woolf, failed to turn up.[42] By this time Ralph Bates must have come to the notice of the British Security Services, because he was stopped on his arrival at Newhaven and his correspondence and manuscripts vetted by Special Branch officers on behalf of MI5.[43]

Ralph Bates returned to Spain once the meeting was over and he was on a walking holiday in the Pyrenees with Winifred when he heard of the General's revolt against the Republican Government of Spain. On 17th July 1936, General Franco, assisted by three other Generals, Mola, Varela and Queipo de Llano, led a military revolt against the democratically elected Spanish Government, thus starting the Spanish Civil War. Ralph and Winifred quickly returned to Barcelona.

Ralph Bates, who was known to Spaniards as El Fantastico because of his incredible energy and his ability to need little sleep, then joined the PSUC, the United Communist and Socialist Party of Catalonia.

> This was a vigil; he was waiting for a dawn that must change life. And the essence of a vigil was belief and profession. When next would he be able to serve the Revolution? He could not hazard a guess. "I believe and I will serve," he murmured.[44]

Having joined the PSUC, Ralph promptly enlisted with the

Republican forces. According to Dr Alan Munton, "He [i.e. Bates] felt that it was necessary to establish concrete associations at a time of political crisis, and this led to his work for the Communist Parties in Spain."[45] I believe, like Alan Munton and H. Gustav Klaus, that Ralph Bates was never a member of the CPGB, though the following short note, included in the FBI files on the writer Ernest Hemingway who was in Spain during the civil war, does show how people may have misinterpreted Ralph's actual situation:

[John Gates] named such men as Louis Fischer, Ralph Bates, Vincent Sheean, and Ernest Hemingway. He referred especially to Fischer's autobiography which slanders the Spanish Communists and the Soviet Union, and Bates referred to speeches attacking the Communist party. Bates also reportedly stated that the Veterans of the Abraham Lincoln Brigade must "boldly expose the partial war policies of the Roosevelt administration".[46]

John Gates (1913–1992, born Solomon Regenstreif) was an American communist journalist who became a Political Commissar in the Lincoln-Washington battalion of the International Brigade. Presumably the term "named" means that Gates named Louis Fischer, Ralph Bates, Vincent Sheean and Ernest Hemingway as being "members of the Communist Party", or, at the very least, communist sympathisers. Louis Fischer (1896–1970) was an American journalist who joined the International Brigade. Vincent Sheean (1899–1975) was also an American journalist, one who covered the civil war for the *New York Herald Tribune*. But the phrase, "Bates referred to speeches attacking the Communist party", is vague. Was Ralph Bates agreeing with, or condemning, these speeches? Although Gates's statement to the FBI is dated 27th April 1943, we should, I think, presume that Gates was referring to a time when he knew Ralph Bates during the civil war i.e. sometime between 1936 and 1938, when, so I imagine, Ralph Bates would have condemned "speeches attacking the Communist party".

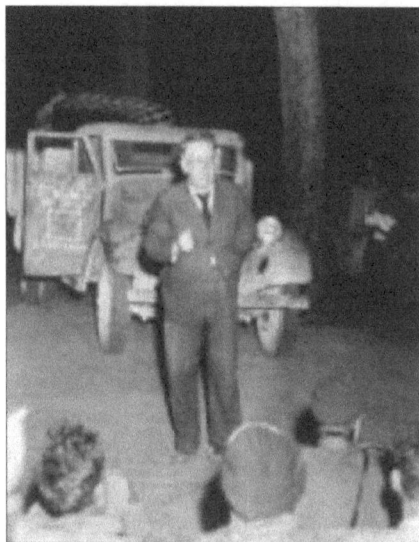

'A *night lecture at the autopark', photograph of Ralph Bates from* Volunteer for Liberty 1, *7 (12 July, 1937), 2.*

Ralph Bates was one of several thousand foreigners who went to help the Republic. It is hard to give exact numbers, although Hugh Thomas, in his monumental two-volume *The Spanish Civil War*, suggests that some 35,000 foreigners went to fight on the Republican side, together with some '10,000 doctors, nurses, engineers and others'.[47] Thomas suggests that there were about 2,000 British volunteers, 'of whom about 500 were killed and 1,200 wounded'.

According to the poet W. H. Auden:

> Many have heard it on remote peninsulas,
> On sleepy plains, in aberrant fishermen's islands
> Or the corrupt heart of a city –
> Have heard and migrated like gulls or the seeds of a flower.

Auden, unlike other writers such as Christopher Caudwell (1907–1937) and Ralph Fox (1900–1937), survived the Civil War.

Why, though, were these people so ready to go to Spain? And why did Ralph Bates become a revolutionary? According to the historian Professor James K. Hopkins:

The influences, then, that turned Bates into a self-professed revolutionary were the result of witnessing the soul-destroying effects of class oppression both in England and Spain. In the beginning, at least, his views had nothing to do with the young British Communist party. But Bates' attitudes began to take on a political character after he arrived in Spain: "I didn't think about theory," he said. What the writer wanted was to live in a society in which the kind of abuse of authority he had known in the British army did not exist. He worked on the docks in Barcelona and irregularly engaged in political organizing. His maturing philosophy, though powerfully felt, did not yet have a center (sic). His belief was that human rights and the dignity of man were inherent and immutable. They could "not be conceded by these people." Moreover, he believed that any society that ignored or abused these rights was to be condemned and fought against, whether in England or Spain. In his own view, the vital power of these convictions "was much more revolutionary than the Communists." In that sense his political stance was "completely anti-ideological," wholly a product of his own experiences and the conclusions he drew from them, although he would hew to the party line during the Spanish war, which included condemning the anti-Stalinist POUM (*Partido Obrero de Unificacion Marxista*) in which (George) Orwell fought.

At first, even with Bates' fluent command of the language, and the work he shared with his Spanish comrades, which included tinsmithing, harvesting olives, and participation in strikes that frequently had the character of a "freeforall," he still found himself

29

not fully taken into their confidence. The issue that crystallized these differences was his friends' refusal to ask him to make a contribution to the needy, perhaps a workman who had caught an arm in a loom or an indigent widow. Although he always volunteered to contribute, it was never requested, which made him feel acutely a sense of a fundamental separateness between himself and his friends and workmates. When he became confident enough to challenge them, they at first offered distracting compliments, but then conceded, "We can't get it out of our heads that you are free and you can go when you want. We can't we're here." There was a difference between them, and Bates saw it.[48]

And Ralph Bates, himself, had this to say on the matter:

Some went in search of personal glory, no doubt; others in search of adventure; a few said they "loved fighting." (The last were all liars, they had merely loved quarrelling: they soon had enough of fighting.) (While) some were endeavouring to integrate themselves…Questioned, even in intimacy, as to their reasons for fighting, very few of these men ever gave an answer, except the stereotyped and uninteresting one, "to fight for democracy."…. There's no doubt whatsoever that they fought for democracy. But the behaviour of plain democrats has been so dissimilar from theirs that I doubt orthodox democracy has power to move men like these.[49]

It was, however, the writer Virginia Woolf who best summed up the feelings of the people left behind. Writing about her nephew, Julian Bell, who went to Spain as an ambulance driver on the Republican side, Woolf said:

I keep asking myself, without finding an answer, what did he feel about Spain? What made him feel it necessary, knowing, as he did, how it must torture Nessa [his mother] to go?...I suppose it's a fever in the blood of the younger generation which we can't possibly understand. I have never known anyone of my generation have that feeling about a war...And though I understand that this is a 'cause', can be called the cause of liberty and so on, still my natural reaction is to fight intellectually; if I were any use, I should write against it...Perhaps it was restlessness, curiosity, some gift that had never been used in private life and a conviction, part emotional about Spain...I'm sometimes angry with him; yet feel it was fine, as all strong feelings are fine; yet they are also wrong somehow; one must control feelings with reason.[50]

Julian Bell died in Spain, at the battle of Brunete, on 18th July 1937, killed when a shell struck his ambulance. He was 29 years old.

Ralph Bates c.1937

Winifred Bates also joined the cause, becoming a journalist, photographer and broadcaster for the *Partit Socialista Unificat de Catalunya* (PSUC). Later she became the personnel officer for the British Medical Aid Unit in Spain, the organisation which had sponsored W. H. Auden's trip to Spain. On one occasion she wrote of the wounded Republicans:

> Men died as I stood beside them. It was summer time and they had been in long training before they crossed the Ebro. Their bodies were brown and beautiful. We would bend over to take their last whispers and the message was always the same; 'We are doing well. Tell them to fight on till the final victory.' It is so hard to make a man, and so easy to blast him to death. I shall never forget the Ebro.[51]

At one point in 1936 Ralph was sent to fight on the front-line:

> One early morning in October, 1936, I sat beside a Catalan militiaman on the Aragon front. We were perched upon a tumbling walltop in Tardienza, gazing, not toward that cursed chapel of Santa Quiteria which had cost the division so many lives, but towards the brown and blue Pyrenees, covered already with a delicate lace of snow. What was going on behind those mountains? What were they thinking of us? What were they doing for us? In particular, what were the revolutionary democrats of America going to do for us?[52]

In December, 1936, Ralph Bates travelled to America to find out for himself just what the "revolutionary democrats of America" could do for the Spanish Republic. His support-raising tour had been organised by the US branch of the League of Writers for Peace and Democracy. According to Ralph's son, Jonathan, Ralph was sent to America, "because of conflicts with the (Communist) Party in Spain.[53] Whilst in America Ralph liaised with members of the North

American Committee to Aid Spanish Democracy, an activist group that supported the Republican side in Spain's Civil War, and also with The Spanish Refugee Relief Campaign. Harold Leon Oram, a journalist with a degree in law, worked for both organisations and he introduced Ralph to Eve Salzman, a fellow member of the Spanish Refugee Relief Campaign. Ralph's 1939 collection of stories about Spain, *Sirocco*, is dedicated to Eve, and the couple were married in 1942, after Ralph had left Winifred.[54]

In January, 1937, Ralph was in New York, when he heard of the death of his friend Ralph Fox:

> I received the tragic news of Ralph's death just before addressing a Madison Square Garden meeting, here in New York. He was one of my best friends. I mean, outside of all questions of political sympathy, he was a man I naturally delighted to be with. Behind all the enormous panoply of that meeting, the vast hall, the gigantic machine of vulgar yet impressive sound passing out of the organ, booming and wailing across the ceiling, the banners of defiance hung around the balcony, the piles of military clothing, the ambulances – behind all the surging excitement that hung before me, there was the remembrance of my friend as I last saw him sitting at my table in London... At that dinner in my flat we fell into excited argument, as we often did. The writing of an encyclopaedia had been proposed by André Malraux. Ralph was enthusiastic, I less so. "No, no, no," I said, "in less than three months we shall have a Fascist rising in Europe." I expected the seat of that rising to be France, yet within three weeks it had broken out and André, Ralph and I were all in Spain.[55]

Ralph Fox, an Oxford graduate who wrote biographies of *Lenin* (1933) and *Genghis Khan* (1936), was perhaps the best-known member of the CPGB to be killed in Spain. He had joined the party in 1926 and, from that point onwards, had tried to make a living as a writer. Fox was a co-founder of the magazine *Left Review* which published some of Ralph Bates's short stories. It seems likely that Ralph Bates saw similarities between himself and Fox:

> Ralph had been longing to go to China. I say longing, because though he had no trace of romanticism in his nature, he never accepted any idea with a merely intellectual and dry assent. I suppose that China for him, as Spain for me, represented two things, escape and reality. Ralph was one of those magnificent fortunate men who escape into reality. He could not go to China, which he already knew and loved. Instead he met his death in Spain.[56]

Ralph Bates returned to Spain in February 1937, and began working in Madrid for the Republican Government's Press Office and the war Commissariat. In April he was sent to Jarama, to the east of Madrid, where he joined the staff of the 97th Spanish Brigade, whose lines were next to those of the British International Brigade volunteers.

> There was one morning on the Jarama front, when we were defending the Valencia road that fed Madrid, the noble heart. I have since written down my memory:
> That morning the four poplars were standing up out of the mist like ship masts, and then, as I mounted the hillside, the other poplars came into view and the valley looked like a harbour into which Mediterranean ships had run...How well I remember that morning. The air ran like invisible, cool water over my face. The light, still striking in beams over the Perales hills, was sharp, crystalline. It was morning when one half believed the open sea lay over the hill...
> As I walked up the gully path, past the telephonic dugout, the

feeling of the sea's nearness made me say aloud to myself, "The crack of an explosive bullet in a gully is like the smack of water in sea caves." At that moment a covey of little brown partridges whirred up out of the red-brown rubble and the beat of their wings sounded like a spent fragment of shell.[57]

Most of the fighting at Jarama had occurred during the period 6th–27th February and things had quietened down somewhat when Ralph was there. The Republican forces at Jarama had included some 450 Americans from the Abraham Lincoln Brigade, who took heavy losses (120 killed, 175 wounded). One Brigade member, the poet Charles Donnelly, commented that, "even the olives are bleeding" before he was killed by machine gun fire.

Donnelly was not the only poet to join the International Brigade. Another poet, the German Eric Bernhard Gustav Weinert (1890–1953), noted that the International Brigade members were creating their own songs to help them in their fight.

Whenever, in the history of the world, freedom has arisen against unfreedom, justice against unjustice, the spirit of the people's uprising has been most clearly and splendidly reflected in its songs, which grew upon the soil of righteous indignation. They were written by the poets who sided with the people; and where there were no such poets the people wrote them themselves…they were created in the middle of the battle, on the firing line, as it were.

Innumerable songs arose during the war of the Spanish people against its enemies. And Spanish was not their only language; for the soldiers of the International Brigade contributed songs, in their own languages, which were loved and became popular among the Spaniards.

No doubt Ralph Bates would have known Eric Weinert's own

piece, 'Song of the International Brigades', with its rousing chorus:

> Forward, International Brigaders, forward!
> Forward, International Brigaders, forward!
> Raise the banner of solidarity.[58]

And Ralph would almost certainly have heard one of the Civil War's best-known songs, 'Jarama Valley', which begins:

> There's a Valley in Spain called Jarama,
> It's a place that we all know so well,
> It is there that we gave of our manhood,
> And so many of our brave comrades fell.[59]

The words were originally written by Alex McDade, of the British Battalion of the 15th International Brigade, who probably heard some American comrades singing the song *Red River Valley*, which employs the same tune. In the second verse mention is made of the British Battalion, which, like the Abraham Lincoln Brigade suffered heavy losses, including the death of the poet Christopher Caudwell, during the battle.

> We are proud of the British Battalion
> And the stand for Madrid that they made,
> For they fought like true sons of the soil.
> As part of the Fifteenth Brigade.

Both the American and German contingents of the International Brigade also sang this song, though they substituted the term "Lincoln Battalion" in the second verse.

There was one song, the spiritual *Go Down Moses*, which Ralph Bates clearly heard, a song sung by black members of the Abraham Lincoln Brigade.

As we ran back with rifles the firing died down and all became silent. "Some guys must have seen an olive tree move," they said. Tired, overstrained senses frequently reported such things. The off-watch men returned to their chabolas or "foxholes" and presently a group began to sing. "When Israel was in Egyptland..."

Their voices swelled out upon the shining night and I say before God that music has never moved me so.

"Let my people go." The voices throbbed out of the earth holes and that sad pleading was more significant than any supplication had hitherto been; it was the voice of the noble heart, giving out the meaning of that bitter fight.[60]

Ralph Bates returned to Madrid sometime in May and began work on a newspaper, *The Volunteer for Liberty*, intended for the English-speaking battalions of the International Brigade, although some issues were also printed in various languages. Bates, assisted by Robert Steck (b.1912, in Illinois) an American member of the International Brigade, edited the first eight issues, with number one appearing in Madrid on May 24th 1937. Another assistant, George Brown (1906–1937) from Salford, Lancashire, (though born in Thomastown, Kilkenny, in Ireland), was later killed at the battle of Brunete. Ralph Bates penned the following tribute:

To the Comrades of the English Battalion – from Volunteer for Liberty

Comrades; it is not the most fitting that one man alone should write what he feels about the loss of our comrade. I have telegraphed to London for a biography of Comrade Brown, but so far it has not arrived. When it does it will be published in full.

George and I slept in the same room while he was stationed here in Madrid. I had never met him before, but we soon became good friends; those who have worked with him will know why. We used often to talk of political work. He always spoke humorously of his own work, but listening to his shrewd accounts and analyses, and feeling his sincerity and steady conviction, one could understand his great worth to the workers' movement.

There was affectionate warmth in Comrade George Brown, combined with a hard and clear understanding that made him a splendid companion in work. Dry and mechanical formality had no place in our comrade, everything was living material, to be handled with sympathy and care. I never saw him treat a single problem as a mere matter of routine. He was always anxious to return to the comrades of the Battalion. I remember how Harry Pollitt, George and I rode down past the North Station in Madrid through the ruined outskirts of the city. That afternoon he told me again that he wanted to get back with you comrades. A day later he came excitedly to me, obviously very happy, and said he was indeed returning to you. We talked a long time on the stairs of this building, over an hour; he had a humorous remark about that also. The next day I was sent to Valencia. When I returned I heard of his death. Well, comrades, you knew him better than we did, but it was a very sad day for us.

The battle for liberty cannot be fought without losses. His was a very great loss. Comrade Lenin once said that for every Communist who falls a hundred will take his place. There will be, there must be, someone who will replace our comrade, because History has signalled us out for Victory. Nevertheless, we mourn him as a grand fighter and as a man. Whoever follows him will have a fine example.

I said that it seemed wrong to me that I should write about Comrade Brown, because he was the battalion's comrade. But I knew him, I knew his great worth and his fine manliness and that is why I have written.

Ralph Bates managed to produce the first eight issues within two months, before being transferred, as a Political Commissar, to the staff of the Fifteenth Brigade. *The Volunteer for Liberty* was then edited by an American, Edwin Rolf (born Solomon Fishman, 1909, died 1954), who was assisted by John Tisa (1919–1991), another American. Tisa, in turn, took over the reins when Edwin Rolfe became ill. Both Rolf and Tisa were, at various times, members of the Communist Party of the USA.

The Fifteenth Brigade, mentioned above in the song *Jarama Valley*, also had its own song, *Viva la Quince Brigada*, which begins:

> *Viva la quince brigada,*
> *Rumba la, rumba la, rumba la,*
> *Viva la quince brigada,*
> *Rumba la, rumba la, rumba la,*
> *Que se ha cubierto de gloria.*
> *¡Ay, Manuela! ¡Ay, Manuela!*
> *Que se ha cubierto de gloria.*
> *¡Ay, Manuela! ¡Ay, Manuela!*[61]
> (Long live the 15th Brigade/They covered themselves with glory.)

It is quite a long song. One verse mentions the difficulties that the Republican forces had at Jarama:

> *En los frentes de Jarama,*
> *Rumba la, rumba la, rumba la,*
> *En los frentes de Jarama,*
> *Rumba la, rumba la, rumba la,*
> *No tenemos ni aviones, ni tanques, ni cañones.*
> *¡Ay, Manuela! ¡Ay, Manuela!*
> *No tenemos ni aviones, ni tanques, ni cañones.*
> *¡Ay, Manuela! ¡Ay, Manuela!*
> (On the Jarama front/We have no airplanes, no tanks, no artillery.)

Political Commissars could, and sometimes did, wield considerable power within the Republican army. However, according to Kenneth Sinclair-Loutit (1913–2003), who met Ralph Bates in Barcelona, this was not always the case.

(Ralph Bates) was wearing a uniform of a deep burgundy colour which displayed no badges or rank-markings. In reply to my enquiry, he said that it was the uniform of a Political Commissar and that his rank was such that it could not be expressed in gold braid. He certainly wore his rank lightly...[62]

Sinclair-Loutit, a Cambridge graduate, was a trainee medical doctor when he went to Spain to help the Republican sick and wounded. He was part of the Spanish Medical Aid Committee (SMAC), formed in Britain in 1936, and was appointed Administrator of the Unit that was sent out to Spain. He was probably introduced to Ralph Bates by Winifred Bates who was, as mentioned previously, the personnel officer for the SMAC.

At times Ralph Bates accompanied Harry Pollitt, the British Communist leader, on the latter's visits to Spain. And Ralph was also called upon to use his organisational skills. On one occasion he stepped in to reorganise the so-called Tom Mann Centuria – one of several autonomous militia groups. The group had been led by the English communist Tom Wintringham, but Wintringham proved an unsuitable leader. According to Richard Baxell, in his book *Unlikely Warriors, The British in the Spanish Civil War and the Struggle Against Fascism* (2012):

The Centuria was visited by Ralph Bates, now working for the Republican government. Despite his appearance, 'tall, stout, about forty, he looked more like a master plumber than a revolutionary leader', he clearly had authority, managing to arrange the replacement of their commander and convincing the disaffected volunteers to join up with another group of English-speaking volunteers, currently training in Albacete.[63]

In July, 1937, Ralph Bates attended the Valencia and Madrid sessions of that year's Congress of the International Association of Writers for the Defence of Culture.

At the time of the International Congress of Writers last July I was allotted a hotel room that was already occupied. The city was so full of refugees that in two hours of search I failed to find a room and at last began to inquire in little cafés in back streets. At last, an old waiter offered to share his bed with me and led me off into the darkness, to arrive at the abandoned palace of some ancient and noble family. Next morning I spent some time wandering through the house, walking in stiff and creaking boots through dark, tapestried salons of the eighteenth century, whose walls were hung with solemn portraits, into rooms decorated in the trinket style of the last century. There were fans of mother-of-pearl filigree and cabinets of carved ivory and portraits of ladies painted in what appeared to be egg tempera, and the floors were of waxed parquet. Presently I came to a library, full of ancient classics, modern paper-backed books by Colette, and a fine edition of Mr. Jorrocks in English. Finally, I came to the Mother Hubbard quarters of the departed menials and, looking through a small square window into the courtyard, I saw a gleaming anti-aircraft gun in this walking through the dead and silent past and coming upon violent but, in this case, merciful modernity.[64]

Following his attendance at the Congress, Ralph was sent to fight in the murderous battle of Brunete, (6th–25th July 1937), where the British Battalion of 300 men were almost all killed.[65] In fact, only 42

41

out of the original 300 survived.

Momentarily blinded, I was seized by a violent fit of coughing, barbs were tearing through my lungs; then, as I flung myself against the river bank I saw a figure blundering down through the dust. "Get down," I yelled, but at that instant another bomb fell. A terrific blast, furnace hot, followed the white flash, then darkness. I thought I was blinded, the skin of my face was peeling off, burnt away; and then I touched it with clay-daubed fingers and opened my eyes. Higher up the bank two bombs crashed. Something huge, black and writhing swept through the air, and I was caught up and hurled backwards into the shallow water.[66]

The following extract, taken from *Of Legendary Time*, is one of the most moving pieces that Ralph Bates ever wrote:

I came down off the black hills one gale-swept night during the Brunete battle, into Villanueva. The town was under shellfire and it was burning. At one moment a blazing roof beam would be flung into the sky, describing a yellow scroll, or a huge inverted cone of sparks would soar up and illuminate the billowing smoke, or a column of flame would rush out and burst above the stubbled fields, sending wave after wave of sparks running down the valley. Within the town, stone and metal were tearing up the air. For safety I entered the church. It was an evacuation station and its floor was covered with wounded men, groaning and screaming....Doctors were going among the men; the church was lit by a few acetylene flares placed in the ground. The long shadows writhed on the walls, like figures in a mobile El Greco. All the church was full of the echoing litany of death. I went up to the dismantled high altar to write my report. Suddenly my imagination, my mind, and my heart were frozen. Bowed over the centre of the altar, his head upon his hands, was a wounded man, blood streaming from his head. He was standing as a priest stands when he murmurs: "Hoc est corpus meum." The man was dying, I thought. He seemed to be pleading the sacrifice of Spain. I stood frozen in imagination, hearing that echoed wailing. Far off the machine guns rattled.

Afterwards I went outside and was sick.[67]

In February, 1937, whilst on his way back to Spain, Ralph Bates was briefly arrested in France for possessing arms, which he was taking to Spain. Ralph's knowledge of the Pyrenees had been used to help the smuggling of arms and personnel into Spain. One person who crossed the mountains this way was Ralph's younger brother, Ronald Bates, who had been told of the Republican struggle by Ralph.[68] Because the French Government had a policy of non-intervention in the Spanish Civil War, Ronald travelled through France under the pretence that he was going on holiday. Having joined the International Brigade, he fought at the battle of Teruel, a town situated between Zaragoza and Valencia, before, in 1938, becoming involved in the Battle of the Ebro, possibly the last great Republican offensive of the Civil War. The situation was such that the Republican soldiers were facing starvation, being far from their supply lines, and they only survived because they found tins of sardines that the Nationalist troops had abandoned. Ronald contracted typhoid and was sent to a small hospital in Barcelona, before being put on the last International Brigade train to leave that city in December, 1938. Back in England, Ronald returned to his Quarry Road home in Swindon, before moving to Reading. He later worked at a home for Spanish refugee children and died, aged 94 years, in 2004.[69]

Meanwhile, as I mentioned above, once Ralph Bates was released from French custody, he moved to Madrid, where he wrote about the armed struggle before returning to America and Mexico, his

Ralph Bates, centre, in Republican uniform. 1st June 1937

Winifred Bates, centre in glasses. Spain 1937?

books and speeches convincing many Americans that they should support the Republican cause. One such person was Junius Scales, an American communist who mentioned Ralph in Mickey Friedman's book *A Red Family: Junius, Gladys and Barbara Scales* (2009).

> But a number of things came along that got me tremendously concerned with Communism. One was the civil war in Spain. It suddenly dawned on me what was going on there. Ralph Bates, the short story writer and novelist who had been in Spain, was on a speaking tour and impressed me tremendously. As a result of his speech and talking with him, I decided I would volunteer to fight against Franco with the International Brigade. The odd thing was that this all happened about the same time I was so anti-militarist, so opposed to compulsory ROTC, and it didn't seem the least inconsistent to me. At this point, though, they were already demobilizing the brigade, so that fell through before it even got started. But the threat of fascism really hit me hard. The Communists seemed to be the consistent anti-Nazis and that further endeared them to me.

Other Americans who joined the International Brigade as a result of reading Ralph Bates's books were Joe Dallett (1907–1937) and Hank Rubin (1916–2011). Rubin published an account of his Civil war experiences and later became a well-known restaurateur in San Francisco.[70]

Ralph Bates was in Toronto, Canada, during the period 8th–12th October 1937. He attended the 8th National Convention of the Communist Party of Canada and spoke at the sixth session before some 450 delegates. The Royal Canadian Mounted Police included this passage in a secret report that had been obtained from either an agent or an undercover officer:

Ralph Bates was introduced as a distinguished British author and Political Commissar of the 15th Column of the International Brigade in Spain. "I want to speak," said Ralph Bates, "not only on behalf of the whole of the Spanish People's Army of which I am a part," in giving a survey of the work of the Republican Army of Spain. Referring to the popular front movement he claimed that "it has been the Spanish Communist Party that has done more than any other organisation, more than any other party to force back International Fascism." He presented a glowing account of the 'People's Army,' stating that it is one of the finest armies in Europe, willing and able to defend itself against any foe. "Before the war," he said, "there was something like 50,000 people in the Spanish Communist Party; today it can claim that 350,000 dues paid members have come into the Party." Speaking on behalf of the International Brigade and of its accomplishments, he said that it saved Madrid. "I want to say that it was the Communist Party of Spain that gave us that unified army, I speak for every man who fought in the firing line, no matter what their political belief may be, when I say that we all have to be grateful to the Communist Party." "When a political party is able to get the masses of the people to follow it, there is proof that its methods are right and the doctrines are right...comrades, I want to say emphatically that for those who are fighting in Spain that the people of Spain, and all the democrats of Spain must, as well as the whole world, stand up and thank the Communist Party of Spain and the Communist International which helped to defend Spain. *Viva la Comintema.*"

On January 19th 1938, Ralph Bates was again in Toronto, where, this time, he addressed a meeting of the Friends of the MacKenzie-Papineau Battalion. Part of another secret report, made by the Royal Canadian Mounted Police who were present at the meeting, has been released:

The Friends of the Mackenzie-Papineau Battalion at Toronto held a mass meeting at the Forester's hall, 22 College Street, on the evening of January 19th. George Watson, recently re-elected President of the Toronto District Trades and Labour Council, acted as Chairman and the speakers were Captain Ralph Bates, A. E. Smith and Beckey Buhay Ewen. Seated on the platform were Rev. Salem Bland, G. Warren Gilroy, Rev. Mr Thomas, Jack Steele, recently returned from Spain and 4 veterans of the Spanish Civil War. The Chairman, after outlining the history of the Committee to Aid Spanish Democracy and the League for Peace and Democracy, called upon Ralph Bates, who spoke from 8.45 p.m. until 11 p.m. eulogizing the Loyalist Army, and the International Brigade in Spain. He admitted that arms were being received by the Loyalists from Mexico and the U.S.S.R., mainly the latter, and strongly defended the acceptance of Russian aid. He, however, denied that there were any Russian troops in Spain. He gave numerous illustrations showing how the United Front had been built up and how it is functioning. He made a vicious attack upon the Spanish Trotskyists devoting almost 20 minutes to the subject. He claimed that the Spanish Army was a democratic army and graphically described, or rather dramatized the suffering of the Spanish people. He also attacked the Roman Catholic Church for siding with Franco, saying that they were betraying the principles of Christianity. He concluded by making a high pressure appeal for donations; the amount collected, however, was not disclosed.

Clearly, Ralph Bates was following the official Party line here by praising Russia while condemning the Trotskyites and the Roman Catholic Church.[71]

And mention of the Catholic Church brings us to an incident which seems to show how Ralph Bates was caught up in events at the beginning of the Spanish Civil War. In October 1936, Ralph produced "a descriptive report" of the destruction of a Spanish church.[72] Declaring that he could neither "condone nor condemn" the action, Bates helped select those church relics which should be saved or burnt. At the end of the piece Ralph states that, "The street is brighter, purer, it seems to Compañero Sagasta, *and to me*, when the church is burnt down."[73]

In this description the church burners are anarchists, another group that Bates felt compelled to denigrate. I have previously mentioned Ralph Bates's description of Anarchism as being, "nothing more than Christianity without God", yet he does consider it important to note that while Compañero Sagasta and his anarchist colleagues are burning the church they take care to ensure that none of the surrounding buildings is damaged. Elsewhere, in *Lean Men* for example, mention is made of Catholic nurses ignoring anarchist and atheist patients, no doubt showing their disapproval of the anticlerical and antireligious stand taken by such people.[74] These writings may suggest that Ralph Bates was sympathetic to anarchists, but this is clearly not the case when we consider this further passage, one describing an anarchist called Sarria, from *Lean Men*.

> The orator, black-shirted and white-faced, was intoxicated with doctrine and emotion, they could make little sense of his utterances. He seemed to vocalize all the wild rumours, all the animal fears and enthusiasms that surged in the collective mentality before him. It really seemed to Francis that Sarria was some kind of loudspeaker for the confused and conflicting hysteria that the last few days had raised. Conscious control of words and thoughts seemed to have disappeared from his speech, he was behaving as the leader of a frustrated wolf-pack might behave. At one minute he would be screaming praises of the "Sacred Revolution", at the next wailing over the loss if brave compañeros, and then without preparation he would fling some impossible proposal before the crowd.[75]

Ralph Bates, like others before him, clearly saw Spanish anarchism as a replacement, or substitute, for the Catholic Church. Indeed, Bates could argue that anarchism was, in itself, a religion:

The psychology of anarchism is religious. Its tragic courage, its total selflessness, its sense of drama, its worship of Action, its fanatical belief in the Myth...its burning, I say burning mystical love for its leaders, its unquestioning obedience, its subtle and amazing intuition, all this, it is evident, discloses anarchism to be a religion.[76]

Nevertheless, despite all his beliefs, Ralph Bates did later admit that many anarchists fought in the Spanish Civil War with complete fearlessness. So much so that Ralph coined a proverb for bravery against all odds. It was "as brave as a Spanish anarchist".

Ralph Bates visited Mexico twice in 1938. His trips were aided by the Mexican Communist Party and by trade union officials. Previously, in 1937, a political tract written by Ralph in Spanish, had been published in Mexico. This was *En la España Leal ha nacido un Ejército* Ediciones de la Sociadad de Amigo de España. Mexico, 1937 (In Spain a Loyal Army was Born). A companion piece, *Unidad proletaria U.G.T.-C.N.T. Las dos poderosas sindacales españolas* Ediciones de la Sociadad de Amigo de España. Mexico, 1938. (Proletarian Unity. The General Union of Workers (U.G.T.) and the National Labour Confederation (C.N.T.), the two powerful Spanish syndicalists), appeared in 1938.

In an inscription written inside a copy of the book *Rainbow Fish*, which Ralph gave to the American writer and editor Dorothy Brewster, we find the sentence, "I'm just setting out for Mexico, where I think I shall be useful." The inscription is dated 2nd February, 1938. Ralph also tells Brewer that, "It was good of you to write that article, and useful, I believe." The "article" may have been Brewster's contribution to the book *Writers Take Side: Letters about the War in*

Spain from 418 American Writers, which was published in New York in 1938 by the League of American Writers. Brewster may have sent a copy of her contribution to Bates prior to publication.

Rainbow Fish contains four stories. The first, *Rainbow Fish*, tells of a group of criminal outcasts working on a boat for a Greek sponge collecting company in order to avoid society and the police. The second, *The Other Land*, is set in London's Pimlico, while the third, *Dead End of the Sky*, is set in France. The final story, *Death of a Virgin*, is a story of Spanish village life.

We know that Dorothy Brewster liked *Rainbow Fish*. She reviewed the book in the New York magazine *Nation*, saying that it was, "As fine a character study as any in recent fiction. It is one of the richest harvests of the new techniques and the new understandings we ascribe roughly to the pioneer work of Joyce and Freud."[77] The English edition of *Rainbow Fish* is dedicated to the English author, critic, playwright and one time literary editor of the *New Statesman*, George Walter Stonier (1903–1985), while the American edition is dedicated to the American author, poet and political activist Corliss Lamont (1902–1995).

Ralph Bates had continued to write books during the Civil War, including the previously mentioned *Rainbow Fish*, published in 1937, and *The Miraculous Horde and Other Stories* (issued as *Sirocco and Other Stories* in America) which was published in 1939. This latter book contained stories about the Civil War and the International Brigade, such as "Jarama Ballad", "Brunete Ballad" and "Guadarrama Ballad", together with the novella *43rd Division*. *Time* magazine had this to say about *Sirocco*, "Ten years ago Ralph Bates was just another energetic, down-and-out, class-conscious workingman, while Ernest Hemingway was an energetic, up-and-coming, self-conscious writing man. Today, Bates's Spanish civil war stories are better than Hemingway's. Bates lived revolution; when it came, he could almost write it with his eyes shut." And a Valentine

Cunningham said of the book, "No one surpassed Bates for nice ironies about the mixed human material in the republican militias, or for moving melancholic reflections on a struggle about which its participants felt increasingly pessimistic."[78]

By 1938 it was becoming clear that Franco's Nationalist troops, supported by Germany and Italy, were beginning to gain the upper hand. The Republic was collapsing and anyone who has read George Orwell's account of the Spanish Civil War, *Homage to Catalonia* (1938), will know how much in-fighting occurred between the various left-wing Republican factions. According to the poet Stephen Spender, who visited Spain at the time of the Civil War, "Bates was an example of a good writer and a good man whom the Communist Party turned into a killer." On one occasion, at the 1937 Madrid Writer's Congress, Ralph Bates admitted to Spender that he had "sent politically unreliable men into a section of the fighting in which (they were) certain to be killed".[79] Orwell, who fought with the anti-Stalinist Worker's Party of Marxist Unification (POUM) having been turned down by the Communists, knew Ralph and Winifred Bates and was highly critical of them. In his book *Homage to Catalonia* Orwell accuses Winifred of saying, in the *Daily Worker,* that the POUM had fewer men than they claimed, thus handing the enemy useful information, and he accuses Ralph of saying, in the *New Republic,* that POUM troops were "playing football with the Fascists in no-man's land". According to Orwell this was, "at a time when, as a matter of fact, the POUM troops were suffering heavy casualties and a number of my personal friends were killed and wounded."

Ralph Bates was clearly affected by the Spanish Civil War and by the in-fighting that took place between the various Republican factions. He was also clearly unhappy with a number of events in late 1939, firstly when, on 28th August, Stalin and Hitler signed the Nazi-Soviet Pact in Moscow, which stated that should either side be involved in a war the other side would remain neutral, and with the Soviet invasion of Finland, which began on 30th November. Bates's response was an article entitled "Disaster in Finland", which appeared in the 13th December 1939, issue of *New Republic*. The article begins with this paraphrasing of the opening line of the *Communist Manifesto*:

> A specter (sic) is haunting the world, the specter (sic) of a revolution that is dead.[80]

and continues with an attack on what has happened, not only in Finland, but throughout Europe. At one point Bates criticises the Spanish POUM's policies, which George Orwell had previously defended.

> The theological bitterness of the (Spanish) Communist Party, however, could be seen in its attitude towards the POUM party. That party's policies would have been disastrous had they been put into effect. That indisputable truth was made the basis for the utterly unscrupulous charge that the POUM was in actual contact with Franco, and was working exclusively and consciously in the interests of the fascists.[81]

Years later Bates said that his actions during the Civil War had been brought about by his first wife, an ardent Stalinist, who had "thoroughly misinformed" him about other left-wing groups fighting in the Civil War.

Ralph Bates, who no longer wished to be a "fellow traveller", ends the article "Disaster in Finland" with the following words:

> Liberals and radicals alike must think hard to work out new projects for the defence and improvement of democracy. It is hard

to lose the affection and respect of so many friends whose bravery and devotion I admire. Nevertheless, I am getting off the train. It will have to be a flying jump, and no doubt the passengers in the compartments behind will shoot at me as they clatter by. I had thought the train was bound for a fertile place in the sun; but I have found out that it is rushing towards the Arctic north, where we will be buried beneath vast drifts of snow and be forever more silent.[82]

And Ralph was correct; the guns were, indeed, lined up against him:

But a pleasant life in America beckoned. His desertion of Winifred was clearly the start of a drift. But the 1939 conflict between the Soviet Union and then fascist-sympathising (sic) Finland, controversy over which was greatly stirred by the UK government, enabled him to denounce the USSR in an article for an American magazine.... His break with the Left was finally absolutely confirmed in 1947 [sic: 1946], when he began a 19 year stint as professor of literature at New York University.[83]

Many people who knew Ralph Bates during the Spanish Civil War described him as being a man of action, the sort of person who, by his actions, could not avoid being criticized by people unable to act like he did. He was probably the sort of person whom Aristotle had in mind when he said, "There is only one way to avoid criticism: do nothing, say nothing, and be nothing." But the time had come, enough was enough, and Ralph Bates left what Arthur Koestler came to call, "an abortive revolution of the spirit, a misfired Renaissance, a false dawn of history".[84] And yet, at the same time, Ralph Bates could write that:

There were times in Spain, moments only as a rule, when my vision of the world was suddenly purified. I mean that it seemed the physical retina itself became more sensitive and that perception, often a mere result of sensation, really felt like a co-operation of the willing and loving mind in the work of the senses. In those moments perception put me in new touch with a world that was lovely, and itself pure. It is hard to describe this sensation but it is the origin of much poetry. I think now, as I thought then, of Thomas Traherne and his "immemorial wheat that never would be reaped." But it was not the permanence of things which I saw so much as the identity of things, their real nature, the glowing serenity that Cézanne could see in the tilt of vineyards and the heavy blue-grey mass of hills beyond the solid cube of a southern house.[85]

Mexico

In 1941 Penguin Books included one of Ralph Bates's short stories *They Required of us a Song* in the anthology Penguin Parade #8. *They Required of us a Song* is unlike Ralph's previous works, in that it tells the story of a Jewish family who settle in the Berkshire village of "Beauchamp St. Michael" and how the death of the Jewish mother affects the Christians of the village. The narrator clearly states that he, "was brought up in the Anglican Church" and as the story progresses we see that he has more than a passing knowledge of Christian church lore. Take, for example, this short exchange between the narrator and the village Squire:

"You admire the sermons of the metaphysical poet, sir," I ventured to say upon the third day of knowing him.

"Indeed I do, and have profit in them, but I would rather read the disquisitions of good Archbishop Laud," he replied. He was, I at once discovered a Laudian High Churchman, and something of an antiquarian in the ceremonies of the Anglican Church. In the church of Beauchamp St. Michael the Sarum Use was followed at the Squire's request. The effect of that Use was of a most pure and solemn dignity; so early English, like the lovely carols of the fourteenth century.

Mention of the "sermons of the metaphysical poet" might suggest that Ralph was talking about Thomas Traherne, who was mentioned above, but further lines suggest that John Donne was actually the poet in question.

Ralph Bates had broken with his communist past. But had he returned to Christianity? As a child playing the church organ he had, presumably, held some form of Christian belief.[86]

But it does seem hard to actually say that he had returned to religion. As Gabriel García Márquez once said, "Disbelief is more resistant than faith because it is sustained by the senses."[87]

When Ralph Bates left Spain, at the end of the Civil War, he returned to Mexico with Eve Salzman, staying in an apartment in Luis Moya Street in Mexico City. At that time Mexico was a country that was willing to take in people from the losing Spanish Republican side.

According to Ralph, Mexico City was the "most banal and cultureless of all the cities I have known".[88] In a long piece, "Conversations in Mexico" he described some of the journeys that he made with Eve, comparing, at times, his own approach to writing with that of D. H. Lawrence and Aldus Huxley.

Lower down the forest overran the ridge. As we entered a glade, sheep broke through the forest wall on the other side, and in a few moments a great flock was bleating around us. For some reason, to see flocks of sheep always creates in me a sense of innocence, of an age of innocence which I know well can never have existed. Perhaps because of long years of study of the Mesta in Spain, of many years of traveling along Sierra tracks, or because of innumerable conversations with shepherds, whose knowledge is traditional, such encounters at once create in me the sense of past time, the feuds of which have been forgotten though its poetry remains. It is an unfailing association, so that on this day, descending out of the pure sky and meeting the flock of sheep, I felt that I was in the Golden Land. Had I thought of writing about Mexico at that moment I believe I should have conceived some mystifying nonsense in the manner of Lawrence or Huxley. But when we entered the forest again we met an Indian shepherd boy, perhaps ten years old. I asked him where the path would lead us and he answered, after a long silence, in the softest of speech. His voice was full of what is called Indian melancholy, the same that haunted his eyes and molded the posture of his body.[89]

It is clear in "Conversations in Mexico" that when it came to Mexican society Ralph Bates sided with the native Indians, whom he called "the dispirited and illiterate dispossessed". In Spain he had detested the Nationalist elite and the Catholic Church. In Mexico it was the outsiders who had come to exploit the Indians and their lands:

The attitude of the directing whites of the Deep South towards the Negro may be appalling, but it is as nothing to the contempt for the Indian and the cynicism as to their own motives displayed by the people who have hitherto owned and governed Mexico. Nor has the Jefe possessed any redeeming feature; cultureless, mannerless, without initiative, he has contributed nothing to Mexico, even during the old regime. A Mexican capitalist's idea of enterprise was to bring out a new aerated water. The gringo, the gachupin, and the ingles were allowed to buy the country and build its major industries. It is the same today….It is these spineless and unbelievably corrupt people and their forebears who have nearly destroyed the Indian's will. Their politicians have used him in revolution, promised him land and water, and time and again they have betrayed him with the most revolting cynicism.[90]

In 1940 Ralph Bates's published another novel, *The Fields of Paradise*. The book's title comes from a mural painted either by David Alfaro Siqueiros (1896–1974), Diego Rivera (1886–1957), or else José Clemente Orozco (1883–1949), of a Mexican village scene. Did Ralph meet with these artists? At least two of these artists, Rivera and Siqueiros, were members of the Mexican Communist Party, and Siqueiros is believed to have been involved in a 1940 plot to assassinate Leon Trotsky, then resident in Mexico. No doubt Ralph would have wanted to meet with them when he visited Mexico in 1938, but it is doubtful if Siqueiros or Rivera would have wanted to meet him after he had written his condemnation of Stalin, *Disaster in Finland*, in late 1939.

In 1940 Ralph Bates also wrote a number of other pieces about Mexico. These included "Mexico in Turmoil", "Developments in Mexico" and "Mexico: Another Spain?"[91] And he also continued to write about Spain, with reviews and articles such as "Postscripts on Spain", "Spain under Franco: Franco's Political Problem" and "The Battle Was Lost in Spain".[92]

New York

Ralph and Eve only stayed in Mexico for a short time before they returned to New York, where they were married. As said above, Ralph had met Eve through knowing Harold Oram and Eve was to remain with the Oram Group Inc. until she retired as a Vice President of the Group. In 1942 Ralph Bates published *The Undiscoverables and Other Stories*. One story, a novella titled *When the Man Comes, Follow Him* was the screenplay for a proposed film that was to be directed by the well-known Fritz Lang. The story was published to confirm copyright, although the film never appeared.[93]

Once settled in New York (the couple lived at 37, Washington Square West, in central Manhattan) Ralph Bates became a staff editorial writer for the New York magazine *Nation*, for which he wrote articles, editorials and book reviews. He also found time to write articles and review books for the *New Republic*.

At 8pm on Wednesday 13th October 1943, Ralph appeared on the popular WHN New York radio program *The Author Meets the Critics*. Started in 1942, the show ran to over four hundred episodes and lasted until 1954. Ralph appeared as a critic. That week's author was Sam Grafton (1907–1997), a New York journalist who had supported the Republican side during the Spanish Civil War. Grafton had worked for such publications as *New Republic, New York Post* and the *Philadelphia Record*. He was also the author of several books, including *All Out! How Democracy will Defend America* (1940) and *An American Diary* (1943). There were also two other critics, Louis Fischer, the same person who was "denounced" to the FBI alongside Ralph Bates and Ernest Hemingway, and who was now working with Ralph at the *Nation*, and Johannes Steel (1908–1988) whose 1934 book *The 2nd World War* predicted that the rise of the Nazis in Germany would bring about a world war.

In 1946, Ralph Bates was appointed Adjunct Professor of Creative Writing and English Literature at New York University. He also occasionally taught non-degree courses outside the University. For example, in October, 1950, Ralph began teaching two courses, "The Literary Approach on Problems of the Self and of Society" and "The Writing of Fiction", at New York's Young Men's and Young

Women's Hebrew Association (YM-YWHA) building in Lexington Avenue.[94]

Ralph continued to support "progressive" organizations. For example, in 1940 he signed an advertisement for the Union of Democratic Action (later Americans for Democratic Action, whose slogan was "anti-fascism, anti-Nazism").[95] The advertisement stated that Ralph was a member of the organizing committee. At some point around 1940 Ralph Bates had also joined the left-wing League of American Writers, an organization founded in 1935 by the Communist Party of the USA (CPUSA), partly to support the Republican faction in the Spanish Civil War. The League lasted until January, 1943, and, while founded by the CPUSA, not all of its members were communists, though many, of course, were.[96] A copy of the League's membership list found its way into the hands of the FBI, who passed it on to the now-infamous House Committee on Un-American Activities, who summoned Ralph Bates to appear before them. He later refused to testify. Of course, any person who had fought for the Republicans during the Spanish Civil War would already have been considered 'subversive' by this Committee! Many people who refused to testify lost their jobs, but Ralph Bates continued to hold his post at New York University, where he remained until he retired as Emeritus Professor in 1966. He did, however, continue to give occasional lectures at the University and he also began building telescopes as a hobby.

One final, semi-autobiographical, novel, *The Dolphin in the Wood* appeared in 1950. The story, set largely in the north Wiltshire village of "Wellingdon Parva", tells of the social changes brought to the village by the Great War. In part, the story can be compared to Flora Thompson's *Lark Rise to Candleford,* or even, at times, to William Cobbett's *Rural Rides.* The book's title is taken from these lines by the Roman poet Horace.:

Who courts variety, and fain would ring
A thousand changes on the selfsame string,
Will paint, as 'twere in fancy's wildest mood,
Boars in the waves and dolphins in the wood.

Towards the end of the book, having failed to marry his childhood sweetheart, we find this statement from the narrator.

Certainty itself flowered. In England I was a dolphin in a wood, wildly out of place. If I tried to live in England I should always be fighting naval battles in a forest. You cannot live with something, with someone you both love and hate, at least not until love and hate have come to seem less important than kindliness and sound judgement. So I would not return but after travel decide where I should live, as myself, which is as much of freedom as a young man can know.

The Dolphin in the Wood is, today, one of the most sought-after of Ralph Bates's book, though this may be due, in part, to the bright, surrealist dust-jacket design that was commissioned from the artist John Minton.[97]

Ralph Bates had been awarded a Guggenheim Fellowship in 1947 and it may be that the award was used to help while he was writing *The Dolphin in the Wood*. Ralph Bates continued to write after this time, but he seems to have considered these later works unfinished. According to his wife, Eve, "There were many things that silenced him in terms of writing and being a public figure. His disillusion with the political scene was complete."[98]

In 1966 Ralph Bates was honoured by the East German Government as the last surviving British author who fought in the Spanish Civil War. At the time of writing, it is not known if he ever returned to Swindon, whether to research or from sentiment, but it is tempting to speculate that he may well have broken a transatlantic journey to re-visit the places of his youth.

Ralph and Eve Bates retired to the Greek island of Naxos, where he climbed until his eighties, only ceasing because of failing eyesight. He became a friend of the German artist Klaus Pfeiffer, who also lived on Naxos, saying that Pfeiffer was, "a precise draughtsman, a brilliant colorist, in part a savage satirist and in part a liberated and joyful fantasist, one whose images create a complex world."

According to a note in the *Swindon Advertiser*, Ralph was delighted when he received a congratulatory card from the Queen on his hundredth birthday. Apparently he had not renounced his British citizenship and had never applied to become an American citizen.

Ralph and Eve had kept an apartment in Manhattan and Ralph died in New York on Sunday, 26th November 2000, aged 101. His ashes were later scattered on Naxos. He was survived by Eve, who celebrated her hundredth birthday in New York on 9th June 2013, and their son, Jonathan, now of Davis, California.[99] I wonder if anyone sang the song *Little Mornings of May*, at Ralph's funeral, a song which Ralph had once called, "that most beloved of Catalan songs".[100]

> Oh the dear little mornings of May
> When the air is a crystal wine
> The small bird maketh sweet joy
> With his warbling so fine
> And the night's cool hissoping
> Maketh the green fields shine.
>
> How happy is this early morning
> Of singing throats and flashing wings
> How sweet to breathe the perfume

Of clustering pines the fresh breeze brings.
While far off in the echoing valley
A labouring peasant sings.

How beautiful to walk this morn
Of scented crystal air
Across the flowered meadow
To see the white flock cropping there
Where softly the cool stream murmurs
Between its banks so green and fair.

Ralph Bates and other writers

We have already seen that Ralph Bates met both the novelist George Orwell and the poet Stephen Spender in Spain, and that Orwell mentions both Ralph and Winifred Bates in his book *Homage to Catalonia*. According to Jennifer Birkett of Birmingham University, Bates also met the English writer Margaret Storm Jameson (1891–1986) in Spain in 1935. Jameson was married to the historian Guy Chapman and would write, among other things, a book about the Spanish Civil War, *No Victory for the Soldier* (1938), which was published as by "James Hill".

> [Margaret Storm Jameson] cut from the first draft of her typescript [of "Journey from the North"] an anecdote about a visit from the writer Ralph Bates, a Communist Party member, who in James Hill's novel would feed in to the figure of the British novelist, Turnbull, a gluttonous, arrogant womaniser who is also a loyal political commissar. Bates, according to the typescript…ate with them in their hotel, told them about the imminence of civil war, which would be, he said, a worker's war, and offered to find a use

for her writing, as an independent voice outside the Party. He had been brought to the Chapmans' flat the year before by Lilo Linke, one evening in 1934, to join Philip Jordan and Nye Bevan at dinner and enlighten them all about Spain: "It's the only country where the movement has kept its soul. Poverty and hard living – that's the secret. You won't see the Labour leaders here stuffing themselves in the Ivy" {101}

Lilo Linke was a German born writer, best-known for her book *Restless Flags: A German Girl's Story* (1934). She later wrote several travel books.[102] Philip Jordan was a war correspondent for the London *News Chronicle* and Aneurin (Nye) Bevan was a Labour politician, who became Minister for Health in the post-war Atlee Government, 1945–1951, and who is remembered today for spearheading the formation of the British National Health Service. Margaret Storm Jameson's use of Ralph Bates as a template for "Turnbull" is interesting, although we can only wonder to what extent she really saw Bates as such an unattractive character.

In 1937 the painter and writer Wyndham Lewis published *The Revenge for Love*, which concerns the period just prior to the Spanish Civil War. The book is critical of the communists in Spain and presents English intellectual fellow-travellers as "deluded". According to Dr Alan Munton, Wyndham Lewis "drew on (the novel *Lean Men*) and on Bates's tough political personality" to create the character Percy Hardcaster in *The Revenge for Love*.[103]

We also know that one other writer, Malcolm Lowry (1909–1957) had read at least two of Ralph Bates's novels, *The Olive Field* and *The Fields of Paradise* and that, according to The Malcolm Lowry Project, an on-line study program organised by members of Otago University in New Zealand, Lowry used direct quotes from *The Fields of Paradise* in his novel *Under the Volcano*.[104]

Afterword

Ralph Bates' final book, *The Dolphin in the Wood*, was published in 1950. There was then a six year gap before he published what may have been his final piece, a review of *The Mozart Companion* edited by H. C. Robins in the *New York Times Book Review*.[105] In 1963 two of Ralph's previously published pieces were included in Robert Payne's book *The Civil War in Spain 1936–1939*.[106] These were 'Brunete Ballad', reprinted under the title 'Brunete', which had first appeared in the 1939 book *Sirocco and other stories*, and 'Of Legendary Times', reprinted as 'Envoi: Of Legendary Times', which was published in 1939, in the *Virginia Quarterly Review*. In 1966 New York's Washington Square Press issued a new edition of *The Olive Field* and a paperback edition appeared twenty years later, issued by The Hogarth Press in London. As Ralph Bates was living in Washington Square in 1966 I do wonder if he was connected professionally with the Washington Square Press, which was founded in 1959.

In 1997, Ralph Bates's tale '43rd Division', a 'story placed in the cursed mountains of the Spanish Pyrenees', was reprinted in Robert H. Bates's University of New England Press book *Mystery, Beauty, and Danger: The Literature of the Mountains and Mountain Climbing*, published in England before 1946. The story had previously appeared in the 1939 book *Sirocco*, where the quotation given above may be found.

I say that the 1953 Mozart review may have been Ralph Bates' final published work because I have heard that, while living on Naxos in 1970, Ralph produced some kind of guide to the island, possibly a guide to walking and climbing on the island. The following, titled "Walking on the paths of central Naxos" by Lefteris Karystineos, is an extract from a Naxos Red Guide:

The best and most suitable way to find out about the landscapes of the Greek islands is walking. In this way we will discover Naxos' hidden charm that doesn't seem to have changed a lot since the Ralph Bates' (1970) vivid description, who used to be a valued scout in our attacks.[107]

We do, however, know that there is an unpublished book about the island, *Naxos Diary*, as well as an unpublished collection of poems, *The Winged Mountain*, that Bates had also written on Naxos.[108]

Following Ralph Bates's death, his papers and related items were left to Yale University. They are now housed in the Beinecke Rare Book and Manuscript Library, P. O. Box 208240, New Haven, CT. 06520-8240. The collection comprises:

Correspondence with literary colleagues and family, most from the 1960s to the 1990s; drafts and reviews of novels and short stories, from the 1960s to 2000; writings of others about Bates, most 1980s-1990s; audiocassettes of lectures by Bates about literature, 1960s-1970s,and interviews with him about his life and writings, 1980s; personal papers, including biographical information and legal documents, 1930s-1970s; a few photographs and documents concerning his International Brigade service during the Spanish Civil War; and materials relating to Jonathan Bates's imprisonment in Syria, 1972-1974, including correspondence with American and Syrian officials, legal documents, notes, and clippings.

Other sound recordings of Ralph and Eve Bates are held in the archives of the Oram Group in New York.

According to some sources, when it came to books about Spain, Ralph Bates was the finest writer of his generation, better even than Hemingway or Malraux.[109] Sad, then, that none of his books remain in print. As I read his books I was reminded of the works of two other English writers. The first is Gerald Brenan, whose book *The Spanish Labyrinth* (1943) dealt with the Spanish Civil War, whilst another book, *South from Granada* (1957), tells of a long-vanished rural community. The second writer is Norman Lewis, whose book *Voices of the Old Sea* (1984) explains how a small Spanish fishing village community was changed beyond recognition by the arrival of mass tourism in the late 1940s.

Bates, Brenan and Lewis all knew and loved Spain and its people. But today Ralph Bates is all but forgotten, which is sad because he had so much to say about the world that he knew and cared for. I can only hope that it will not be too long before some of Ralph Bates' books are back in print again.

Bibliography of books, stories and related items by Ralph Bates

Books:

1 by Ralph Bates

Sierra. Peter Davies, London. 1933

Lean Men: An Episode in a Life. Peter Davis, London. 1934

Franz Schubert. Peter Davies, London. 1934

The Olive Field. Jonathan Cape, London. 1936

Rainbow Fish: Four Short Novels. Jonathan Cape, London. 1937

Sirocco and other Stories. Random House, New York. 1939. Reprinted, in somewhat different form, as *The Miraculous Horde and Other Stories*. Jonathan Cape, London. 1939.

The Fields of Paradise. E. P. Dutton, New York. 1940

The Undiscoverables and other Stories. Random House, New York. 1942. (*The Undiscoverables* first published in nine parts in the *Nation* (New York) in 1941.)

The Dolphin in the Wood. Rupert Hart-Davies, London. 1950

2 Containing work by Ralph Bates

Frank Pitcairn (Pseudonym of Claude Cockburn) *Reporter in Spain*. With an Introduction by Ralph Bates. Lawrence & Wishart, London, 1936

"My Friend, Ralph Fox" – in *Ralph Fox: A Writer in Arms* edited by John Lehman, T. A. Jackson and C. Day Lewis. Lawrence & Wishart, London, 1937

Stories and Related Items:

"Miscellany: Serenade to Bankruptcy" – short story in *Time and Tide* XV, 43 (27 October 1934), 1351–1352

"Miscellany: Elephants in Bloomsbury" – short article in *Time and Tide* XVI, 14, (6 April 1935), 491–492

"The Secret" – short story in *Left Review* 1, 7 (April 1935), [247] -252, 254

"Mediterranean Night" – short story in *New Statesman and Nation* N.S. X, 246 (9 November 1935), 681–682

"The Launch" – short story in *New Writing* 1, (Spring 1936) 1–7

"Comrade Vila" – short story in *New Writing* II (Autumn 1936), 38–51

"Compañero Sagasta Burns a Church" – short story in *Left Review* II, 13 (October, 1936), [681]–687

"Death of a Virgin" – novella in *Story Magazine* X, 8 (May 1937)

"Forty-Third Division: A Story in Two Parts. Part I", *Harper's Monthly Magazine* 178, 1 (December 1938), 49–59

"Forty-Third Division: A Story in Two Parts. Part 2", *Harper's Monthly Magazine* 178, 2 (January 1939), 205–216

"Of Legendary Time" – essay in *Virginia Quarterly Review* XV, 1 (Winter 1939), 21–36. (Reprinted in Robert Payne *The Civil War in Spain 1936–1939* Secker & Warburg, London.1963. This book also includes the story "Brunete", first printed in the book *Sirocco and other Stories*)

"Conversation in Mexico" – short story in *Virginia Quarterly Review* XV, 3 (Summer 1939), 393–407

"The Burning Corn" – short story in *Virginia Quarterly Review* volume 15, number 4, Autumn, 1939. University of Virginia, Charlottesville, VA.

"They Required of us a Song" – short story in Penguin Parade #8, Penguin Books, Harmondsworth. 1941

"Journey to the Sandalwood Forest" – story in *Tomorrow* VII, 2 (October 1947), 24–31. Ends with the note (To Be Continued), but this is the only known part

"The Twelfth Basket" – story in *Tomorrow* VII, 11 (July 1948), 39–45

"In Shining Naxos – pages from a diary" – introduction by Vincent Giroud, in *Yale Review* volume 91, number 4, 2003. Yale University Press

This bibliography omits the many book reviews and short political tracts that were written by Ralph Bates. For a comprehensive listing of these, see Alan Munton and Alan Young *Seven Writers of the English Left: A Bibliography of Literature and Politics, 1916–1980*. New York and London: Garland Publishing Inc., New York and London, 1981. pp. 83–115

Notes and references

1 Clive Carter, "Swindon in the Age of Farming", *Swindon Heritage* 4 (Winter, 2013), 49.

2 Ralph Bates obituary in *The Volunteer: The Journal of the Veterans of the Abraham Lincoln Brigade*, New York. Vol. XXIII, No. 5, (Winter, 2001).

3 Ralph Bates, *The Dolphin in the Wood*, London: Rupert Hart-Davis, 1950, p.24.

4 In the introduction to Frank Pitcairn (actually Claude Coburn), *Reporter in Spain*, Laurence & Wishart, 1936, p. 7, Ralph Bates is described as "formerly in the N.U.R".

5 Reported by the local Swindon television station Swindon Viewpoint. I am told by someone who knew Ralph Bates that Bates was extremely proud of his Swindon background and that he never forgot his early work in the GWR factory. There are two photographs of the "O" shop, showing the drive belts and the high ceiling struts, in Tim Bryan's *Great Western Swindon*, Stroud: Tempus Books, 1995, p. 29.

6 *The Dolphin in the Wood* p. 72.

7 *ibid.* p. 76.

8 Paul Joseph Melia, *You Sons and Strangers: lesser-known British writers in the Spanish Civil War*. Unpublished Doctoral dissertation, University of Salamanca, 2013. Accessed on-line 22.4.14. The Ralph Bates' quotations are from *The Dolphin in the Wood*, pp. 76–77.

9 *The Dolphin in the Wood*, pp. 76–77.

10 Paul Joseph Melia, op cit.

11 H. Gustav Klaus, 'Homage to Catalonia: the Fiction of Ralph Bates', *London Magazine*, volume 28, 11–12, (1989), p. 48.

12 *The Dolphin in the Wood*, p. 164.

13 Valentine Cunningham, The *Guardian* newspaper, 12th December 2000.

14 Valentine Cunningham, in the Introduction to *The Olive Field*, London: The Hogarth Press, 1986.

15 H. Gustav Klaus, "Homage to Catalonia: the Fiction of Ralph Bates", *London Magazine*, volume 28, issue 11–12, (February, 1989), 45–56.

16 *ibid.* The town of Sabadell lies a few miles to the north of Barcelona.

17 These and other GWR records are now housed in the Swindon and Wiltshire Archives in Chippenham.

18 Roughly £75 in today's money.

19 Alan Munton & Alan Young, *Seven Writers of the English Left: A Bibliography of Literature and Politics, 1916–1980*, New York & London: Garland Publishing Inc., 1981, p.84.

20. H. Gustav Klaus, "Homage to Catalonia: the Fiction of Ralph Bates", *London Magazine*, volume 28, issue 11–12, (February, 1989), 45–56.

21 Ralph Bates obituary in *The Volunteer: The Journal of the Veterans of the Abraham Lincoln Brigade*, New York, Vol. XXIII, No. 5, (Winter 2001).

22 Ralph Bates, *Lean Men*, London: Peter Davis, 1934, p.166. Ralph Bates's grandfather, Alfred William Bates (b.1832), married Mary Comer Roy (1837–1908) in 1855. Mary's father, Ralph's great-grandfather, was James Roy (1809–1850). His family seem to have been "beer agents" who imported foreign beers into England. James is believed to have died in Amberg-Sulzbach, Bavaria, Germany. Could it be that, over the years, the Bates family somehow or other turned James Roy into someone involved in the Spanish sherry trade, rather than the beer trade? Or was there another member of the Roy family who did die in Spain?

23 Ralph Bates, *Sirocco and other stories*, New York: Random House, 1939, p.166.

24 King Alfonso XIII left Spain in April, 1931.The ploughman's song, known in Spanish as a *saeta*, forms the basis for Chapter 2 of Bates's novel *The Olive Fields* (1936). An outstanding *saeta* performance was captured in Seville by Radio Nacional, of Madrid, and can be heard on the Rounder CD *The Alan Lomax Collection Sampler* (CD 1700). Bates misspells the name of Navalonguilla.

25 Introduction to *Reporter in Spain* by Frank Pitcairn (Claude Cockburn), London: Lawrence & Wishart, 1936.

26 I say "apparently" because I am unable to find a record of their marriage in the General Register Office for England. If they married abroad, in Spain for example, then there would be no UK record of this event.

27 For more on this, see David Callaghan, 'Negotiating Spanish Poets in England, 1920–1940'. Available at http://www.academia.edu/706141/ Negotiating Spanish Poets in England 1920 1940. Accessed 4.5.2014.

28 My copy of *Lean Men* carries the written inscription, "To my dear friend Walter Greenwood, with gratitude. Ralph Bates". Walter Greenwood (1903–1974) was the author of the novel *Love on the Dole*, which was published in 1933. Greenwood's novel was later adapted into a stage play and a film.

29 In 1938 Penguin Books published a two-volume paperback version of *Lean Men*. It apparently sold well.

30 For example, Schubert's father was a school assistant, his mother a domestic servant. Interestingly, a copy of Bates's *Franz Schubert* was sold at auction by Christies-NY during a sale held October 28th–29th 1999. It was from the library of Marilyn Monroe.

31 "Man's life's a vapor, and full of woes/He cuts a caper, and down he goes".

32 I am aware that Ralph Bates reviewed the following music books: William Murdoch's *Chopin: His Life* (1934), Margaret H. Glyn's *The Theory of Musical*

Evolution (1934), Percival R. Kirby's *The Musical Instruments of the Native Races of South Africa* (1935), John Foulds' *To-day: Op. 92* (1935), Sir Walford Bavies' *The Pursuit of Music* (1935), Werner Wolff's *Anton Bruckner: Rustic Genius* (1942), Henri Prunières' *A New History of Music: The Middle Ages to Mozart* (1943), B. H. Haggins' *Music for the Man Who Enjoys 'Hamlet'* (1944), Bishop Fan S. Noli's *Beethoven and the French Revolution* (1948) and H. C. Robbins' *The Mozart Companion* (1956). Dates in parenthesis are review dates and not necessarily dates of book publication. Ralph Bates also wrote a short article about Spanish guitar music, "Listening to Spain", which was published in *Listener* XV, 382 (6 May 1936), 895 – 896.

33 In Stanley Weintraub's *The Last Great Cause: The Intellectuals and the Spanish Civil War*, London: W. H. Allen, 1968, p.291, we are told that, "*The Olive Field* had to be sent to him (Bates) in galley proof in Spain, where he was already so politically active during the months which preceded the civil war that he was unable to read it – and the galleys had been set by Cape from a typescript he had never seen, one made in England from the hand-written manuscript he had left behind." Because of this, a number of corrections were made in the second edition of 1966.

34 Ralph Bates, "Of Legendary Times", *Virginia Quarterly Review*, XV, 1 (Winter), 1939.

35 Valentine Cunningham, in the Introduction to the 1986 edition of *The Olive Field*. London: The Hogarth Press.

36 See, for example, *Lorca's Gypsy Ballads (Romancero gitano)*, published in 1928.

37 *The Olive Field*, Chapter 2.

38 *ibid*, Chapter 32.

39 According to Raimund Schäffner, Bates mentioned this sequel in a letter to H. Gustav Klaus. See H. Gustav Klaus & Stephen Knight (eds), *To Hell With Culture: Anarchism and Twentieth-Century British Literature*, Cardiff: University of Wales Press, 2005, p. 79.

40 H Gustav Klaus, *The Literature of Labour. Two Hundred Years of Working Class Writing*. Brighton: Harvester Press, 1985, p. 115.

41 Valentine Cunningham, the *Guardian*, 12 December, 2000.

42 For an account of this meeting, see *Left Review* Volume 2, number 10, July, 1936.

43 See James Smith's *British Writers and MI5 Surveillance, 1930–1960*. Cambridge University Press, 2012.

44 *Lean Men*. New York, 1935. p. 554.

45 Alan Munton & Alan Young, *Seven Writers of the English Left. A Bibliography of Literature and Politics, 1916–1980*, New York & London: Garland Publishing Inc., 1981, p.84.

46 www.poetry.rapgenus.com accessed 14.1.14.

47 Hugh Thomas, *The Spanish Civil War* 2 volumes.1961. My revised edition published by the Folio Society, London. 2014.

48 James K. Hopkins, *Into the Heart of the Fire*, Stanford University Press, 1998.

49 Review of *The Last Volunteers* by Edwin Rolfe. New York, Random House, 1939, in *The New Republic* December 27th, 1939, p. 293.

50 Quoted in Hugh Thomas, *The Spanish Civil War*. My edition, The Folio Society, London, 2014. Volume 2, 560.

51 Original source unknown. The passage is quoted in several secondary sources.

52 Review of *The Last Volunteers* by Edwin Rolfe. New York: Random House, 1939, in *The New Republic* December 27th, 1939, p. 293.

53 Ralph Bates obituary in *The Volunteer. The Journal of the Veterans of the Abraham Lincoln Brigade*, New York: Vol. XXIII, No. 5 (Winter), 2001.

54 Some sources give the name of Bates's second wife as Eve Haxman. Winifred Bates returned to England and became a shop assistant in the Co-op, before getting a job in Manchester Corporation's Electric Works. At times she taught Esperanto. She later remarried and remained a communist until her death in 1996.

55 John Lehmann, C. Day Lewis & T. A. Jackson (eds), *Ralph Fox. A Writer in Arms* London: Lawrence & Wishart, 1937, pp. 8 – 9.

56 *ibid.*

57 Ralph Bates. 'Of Legendary Time', *Virginia Quarterly Review*, Virginia Quarterly Review, XV, 1 (Winter), 1939.

58 For a recording of "Song of the International Brigades", see *Songs of the Spanish Civil War*: 1. Smithsonian Folkways Archival records (FH5436), Washington. Eric Weinert was a member of the International Brigade from 1937 until 1939. His Spanish Civil War poems were published in Germany, in 1951, under the title *Camaradas*. The poems are in the German language. It is sometimes said that, although the Nationalists won the Spanish Civil War, the Republicans had the better songs!

59 *ibid.*

60 Ralph Bates, 'Of Legendary Time', *Virginia Quarterly Review*, XV, 1 (Winter), 1939.

61 *ibid.*

62 Kenneth Sinclair-Loutit, *Very Little Luggage* 2009.

63 The quote "tall, stout, about forty...etc" is from Keith Scott Watson, *Single to Spain*. London: Arthur Baker, 1937, p.82. Watson, originally an English journalist, was a member of the International Brigade.

64 Ralph Bates, "Of Legendary Time", *Virginia Quarterly Review*, XV, 1 (Winter), 1939.

65 In 1987 the fiftieth anniversary of the Writer's Congress was celebrated in

Valencia. Ralph Bates was not invited.

66. Ralph Bates, "Brunete Ballad", *Sirocco*, Random House, New York, 1939.

67 "Of Legendary Time" *Virginia Quarterly Review*, XV, 1 (Winter), 1939.

68 Like Ralph Bates, Ronald Bates had worked in the GWR factory in Swindon. Apparently there were a number of Spanish Republican supporters working at the factory and, according to the late Brian Bridgeman of the Swindon Society, "Employees from the railway works were involved in an operation to convert a motor van into an armour-plated ambulance which was then sent to the Republicans. In the early works there was this group of people who wanted to send aid to Spain but they were unpopular and called communists. At the time this sort of thing was frowned upon and people were secretive about what they did." According to another Swindon resident, Ken Gibbs, who was a young boy at the time, "I remember standing at the front gate of our house in Montague Street with my father waiting for something which turned out to be this ambulance which he said was going to Spain. As I recall the vehicle was probably an ordinary van that had been converted and was covered in places with steel sheet. I understand it had been financed by the local Communist Party and fitted out by them. I clearly remember seeing it driving along the road showing the people of the area what had been purchased and what was being done towards the medical requirements for the Spanish Republicans. It was a smallish van with red crosses painted on... there was a lot of support for the Communist Party in those days and it was likely that the skill and expertise of rail workers had been used to convert the vehicle. I believe the vehicle was purely a local effort and that it was probably driven to the coast, put on a container and shipped to Spain." (The Volunteer. *The Journal of the Veterans of the Abraham Lincoln Brigade*, New York. Vol. XXIII, No. 5 (Winter), 2001.)

69 Another of Ralph Bates's brothers, Leslie Alfred Bates, became a member of the CPGB and was active within the Swindon branch of the Amalgamated Engineering and Electrical Union (AEU). According to a fellow Communist, Les once told him that, as a young man, Ralph Bates had gone to Montana, where he joined the Industrial Workers of the World (IWW, often known as the "Wobblies"). There Ralph worked organising a union in the copper mines, but a comrade was murdered by the mine bosses and Ralph was told to leave, otherwise he would be thrown down a mine shaft. (Personal communication, 22.12.13) I do rather wonder if this apocryphal tale was based on the story of IWW member, and political song-writer, Joe Hill (1879 –1915), who was executed in Utah on a trumped-up murder charge. The song *Joe Hill* (which begins with the lines: I dreamed I saw Joe Hill last night/Alive as you and me/Says I, "But Joe, you're ten years dead"/I never died says he, I never died says he) became extremely popular within British left-wing groups from the 1940s onward. Les Bates was remembered by the AEU in Swindon by having a room named the Les Bates Hall in their building.

70 Hank Rubin, *Spain's Cause was Mine*. Southern Illinois University Press, 1997.

71 It should, perhaps, be mentioned that, at the time of the Spanish Civil War the Catholic Church was the largest land-owner in Spain. As such it was totally against the Republican Government's land-reform policies.

72 "Compañero Sagasta Burns a Church", *Left Review* II, 13 (October, 1936), p. 687.

73 My italics. But Ralph may have had a change of heart some years later in Mexico. "One day I was in the town of Actopan, photographing some very realistic statues of the suffering Christ." ("Conversation in Mexico", *Virginia Quarterly Review* XV, 3 (Summer 1939) p. 395.)

74 *Lean Men* p. 77.

75 *ibid*. p.311.

76 Ralph Bates "Compañero Sagasta Burns a Church", *Left Review* II, 13 (October, 1936), p. 685. Those wishing to know more about Ralph Bates's attitude to anarchism should consult Raimund Schäffner's essay, "Ralph Bates and the Spanish Anarchists in *Lean Men* and *The Olive Field*", in H. Gustav Klaus & Stephen Knight (eds) "To Hell With Culture" *Anarchism and Twentieth-Century British Literature*, Cardiff: University of Wales Press, 2005, pp. 66 – 81. Schäffner describes Ralph Bates as a little known but "outstanding communist propagandist, journalist and novelist". The two quotations given above from *Lean Men* (footnotes 42 & 43) come from this essay.

77 Quoted on the dust jacket of Ralph Bates's novel *The Fields of Paradise* New York: E. P. Dutton & Co.,1940.

78 Valentine Cunningham, in Ralph Bates's obituary, the *Guardian*, 12 December, 2000.

79 Stephen Spender *World Within World* (1957). Spender does not actually name Ralph Bates. Spender uses the phrase "an English Communist novelist", but as Ralph Bates was the only "English Communist novelist" left fighting in Spain there can be no doubt who Spender was referring to.

80 "Disaster in Finland", New Republic CI, 1306, (13th December, 1939), 221–225. The Communist Manifesto begins with the famous words, "A spectre is haunting Europe, the spectre of communism".

81 *ibid*. p.224.

82 *ibid*. p.225.

83 www.grahamstevenson.me.uk accessed 12.1.14. Ralph Bates began work at New York University in 1946. One occasionally sees the years 1947 or 1948 given in various publications as his start date.

84 Arthur Koestler, in Richard Crossman (ed), *The God That Failed: Six Studies in Communism*. London, 1950.

85 Ralph Bates, "Of Legendary Time", *Virginia Quarterly Review*, XV, 1 (Winter), 1939. Thomas Traherne (1636 or 1637–1674) was a member of the clergy,

famed for his metaphysical poetry. The line quoted here comes from his *Centuries of Meditations* (3rd Century, section 3), which was written c. 1672 though not published until 1908. The full quotation actually reads, "The corn was orient and immortal wheat, which never should be reaped, nor was ever sown. I thought it had stood from everlasting to everlasting." I find it interesting that Ralph Bates should quote Traherne in a passage that reminds me of the writings of many Buddhist mystics

86 However, in the "autobiographical" novel *The Dolphin in the Wood* the narrator says, "Parish organist from my thirteenth year, I was never much of a one for religion." Later, having survived fighting in the Great War, the narrator says, "the real truth was that I couldn't square war with a religion I didn't believe". And, in his other "autobiographical" novel *Lean Men* we find a similar line, again spoken by the novel's narrator, "Some astonishment at discovering that my religion had disappeared unobserved."

87 Gabriel García Márquez *Of Love and Other Demons* (1994).

88 "Conversation in Mexico", *Virginia Quarterly Review* XV, 3 (Summer 1939) pp. 398.

89 *ibid.* pp. 393 – 407. The "Mesta" was a powerful Medieval Spanish association of sheep ranchers.

90 *ibid.* p. 399. "Jefe" is a Spanish word meaning "boss" or "chief". A "gapuchin" is a Spanish settler, while "ingles" refers to English, or British, settlers.

91 'Mexico in Turmoil', *New Republic* 102, 2 (8th January, 1940) p.459. 'Developments in Mexico', *Nation* 151, 11 (14th September 1940), p.202. 'Mexico: Another Spain', *Nation* 151, 11, (14th September, 1940) pp. 210–213.

92 'Postscripts on Spain', *Saturday Review of Literature* XXII, 3 (11th May, 1940), p. 6 & 15. 'Spain Under Franco: Franco's Political Problem', *New Republic* 102, 20 (13th May, 1940), pp. 636 – 638. 'The Battle Was Lost in Spain', *New Republic* 102, 25 (17th June, 1940), p. 11.

93 Another story "Journey to the Sandalwood Forest", printed in *Tomorrow* in 1947 was also planned as a story for a film.

94 These courses are advertised in *Partisan Review* volume VVII, number 7, (September-October, 1950). Unnumbered page.

95 The advert was printed in *New Republic* 104, 21 (26th may 1941), p. 740.

96 Many well-known writers joined the League of American Writers. These include: James Agee, Conrad Aiken, W. H. Auden, Albert Einstein, Robert Frost, Martha Gellhorn, Ernest Hemingway, Dashiell Hammett, Langston Hughes, Thomas Mann, Upton Sinclair, John Steinbeck and William Carlos Williams.

97 At least one on-line bookseller had this to say about *The Dolphin in the Wood*, "The surreal and colorful (sic) jacket is the most desirable feature".

98 Eve Bates, quoted on http://www.spartacus.schoolnet.co.uk/TUbatesR.htm

99 In the 1970s Jonathan Bates was imprisoned in Syria, charged with espionage. He was only released when Henry Kissenger became involved.

100 See p. 533 of *Lean Men* for this quotation.

101 Jennifer Birkett 'Margaret Storm Jameson and the Spanish Civil War: The Fight for Human Values' in *Journal of English Studies* Volume 5–6 (2005–2008), 13–29.

102 I now own Lilo Linke's copy of *Lean Men*. It is inscribed "Ralph Bates to Lilo".

103 Alan Munton, in entry on Ralph Bates, in *Encyclopaedia of Literature & Politics: Censorship, Revolution & Writing* (edited by M. Keith Booker), Westport, Connecticut & London :Greenwood Press, 2005, volume 1, p. 69.

104 www.otago.ac.nz/englishlinguistics/lowry/contents/parent accessed 1.10.13.

105 *New York Times Book Review*, 5th August, 1956, p.5.

106 Robert Payne, *The Civil War in Spain 1936–1939*. London: Secker and Warburg, 1963.

107 http://naxos.redguidebooks.gr/uploads/media/Where To Go 03.pdf accessed 4.5.14.

108 Extracts from *Naxos Diary* have been published in *The Yale Review* Volume 91, number 4. October, 2003.

109 See, for example, Hemingway's *For Whom the Bell Tolls* (1940), or Malraux's *L'Espoir* (1937), translated as *Man's Hope* (1938).

Acknowledgements

It goes without saying that I could not have written this without help, especially that of Dr Alan Munton, who corresponded with Ralph Bates in1980 and published his findings in two books, *Seven Writers of the English Left: A Bibliography of Literature and Politics, 1916–1980* (with Alan Young), New York & London: Garland Publishing Inc., 1981, and *Encyclopedia of Literature & Politics: Censorship, Revolution & Writing* (edited by M. Keith Booker), Westport, Connecticut & London: Greenwood Press, 2005. I must also thank Dr Munton for reading and correcting an early draft of this book. Any faults which remain are, of course, my own. My thanks also to David Colcombe of Devizes, for help with the Great Western Railway records, and to all the writers and researchers whose words are reproduced in this book. I am also indebted to Frances Bevan, Susan Camburn, Naomi Webb and Frank Weston for help researching the Bates' family genealogy.

Illustrations

Cover studio portrait of Ralph Bates. Original print in author's collection.

Photograph of Morse Street, Swindon. Courtesy of John Walsh, Swindon.

Postcard of Swindon and North Wiltshire Technical Institution in author's collection.

Photographs of Ralph and Winifred Bates taken during the Spanish Civil War courtesy of the Abraham Lincoln Brigade Archives, New York.